Anne Ritchie

Records of Tennyson, Ruskin, Browning

.

Anne Ritchie

Records of Tennyson, Ruskin, Browning

ISBN/EAN: 9783337140908

Printed in Europe, USA, Canada, Australia, Japan

Cover: Foto ©ninafisch / pixelio.de

More available books at **www.hansebooks.com**

ALFRED TENNYSON
From a photograph by the Autotype Company, London

RECORDS OF

TENNYSON, RUSKIN, BROWNING

BY

ANNE RITCHIE

ILLUSTRATED

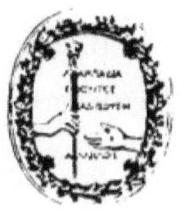

NEW YORK

HARPER & BROTHERS, FRANKLIN SQUARE

1893

" Mind that there is always a certain *cachet* about great men—they speak of common life more largely and generously than common men do—they regard the world with a manlier countenance, and see its real features more fairly than the timid shufflers who only dare to look up at life through blinkers, or to have an opinion when there is a crowd to back it."—*English Humorists.*

"'I remember poor Byron, Hobhouse, Trelawney, and myself, dining with Cardinal Mezzocaldo at Rome,' Captain Sumph began, 'and we had some Orvieto wine for dinner, which Byron liked very much. And I remember how the Cardinal regretted that he was a single man. We went to Civita Vecchia two days afterwards where Byron's yacht was—and, by Jove, the Cardinal died within three weeks, and Byron was very sorry for he rather liked him.'

"'A devilish interesting story, indeed,' Wagg said. 'You should publish some of these stories, Captain Sumph, you really should,' Shandon said."—*Pendennis.*

CONTENTS

ILLUSTRATIONS

ALFRED TENNYSON

> *"A footfall there*
> *Suffices to upturn to the warm air*
> *Half germinating spices ; mere decay*
> *Produces richer life ; and day by day*
> *New pollen on the lily-petal grows,*
> *And still more labyrinthine buds the rose."*
>
> SORDELLO.

THERE is a place called Somersby in Lincolnshire, where an old white rectory stands on the slope of a hill, and the winding lanes are shadowed by tall ashes and elm-trees, and where two brooks meet at the bottom of the glebe field. It is a place far away from us in silence and in distance, lying upon the "ridgèd wolds." They bound the horizon of the rectory garden, whence they are to be seen flowing to meet the sky. I have never known Somersby, but I have often heard it described, and the pastoral country all about, and the quiet, scattered homes. One can picture the rectory to one's self with something of a monastic sweetness and quiet; an ancient Norman cross is standing in the church-yard, and perhaps there is still a sound in the air of the bleating of flocks. It all comes before one as one reads the sketch of Tennyson's native place in the *Homes and Haunts of the British Poets:* the village not far from the fens, "in a pretty pastoral district of softly sloping hills and large ash-trees. . . . The little glen in the neighborhood is called by the old monkish name of Holywell." Lord Tennyson sometimes speaks of this glen, which he remembers white with snow-drops in their season; and who will not recall the exquisite invocation:

"Come from the woods that belt the gray hill-side,
 The seven elms, the poplars four
 That stand beside my father's door,

And chiefly from the brook that loves
To purl o'er matted cress and ribbèd sand,
Or dimple in the dark of rushy coves. . . .
    O! hither lead thy feet!
Pour round mine ears the livelong beat
Of the thick-fleecèd sheep from wattled folds,
    Upon the ridgèd wolds."

The wind that goes blowing where it listeth, once, in the early beginning of this century, came sweeping through the garden of this old Lincolnshire rectory, and, as the wind blew, a sturdy child of five years old with shining locks stood opening his arms upon the blast and letting himself be blown along. and as he travelled on he made his first line of poetry and said, " I hear a voice that's speaking in the wind," and he tossed his arms, and the gust whirled on, sweeping into the great abyss of winds. One might, perhaps, still trace in the noble, familiar face of our Poet Laureate the features of this child, one of many deep-eyed sons and daughters born in the quiet rectory among the elm-trees.

Alfred Tennyson was born on the 6th of August, 1809. He has heard many and many a voice calling to him since the time when he listened to the wind as he played alone in his father's garden, or joined the other children at their games and jousts. They were a noble little clan of poets and of knights, coming of a knightly race, with castles to defend, with mimic tournaments to fight. Somersby was so far away from the world, so behindhand in its echoes (which must have come there softened through all manner of green and tranquil things, and, as it were, hushed into pastoral silence), that though the early part of the century was stirring with the clang of legions, few of its rumors seem to have reached the children. They never heard at the time of the battle of Waterloo. They grew up together playing their own games, living their own life; and where is such

TENNYSON'S BIRTHPLACE, SOMERSBY RECTORY, LINCOLNSHIRE

Drawn by Alfred Parsons, after photograph by Carlton & Sons, Horncastle

life to be found as that of a happy, eager family of boys and girls before Doubt, the steps of Time, the shocks of Chance, the blows of Death, have come to dim or shake their creed?

These handsome children had beyond most children that wondrous toy at their command which some people call imagination. The boys played great games like Arthur's knights; they were champions and warriors defending a stone heap, or again they would set up opposing camps with a king in the midst of each. The king was a willow wand stuck into the ground, with an outer circle of immortals to defend him of firmer, stiffer sticks. Then each party would come with stones, hurling at each other's king, and trying to overthrow him. Perhaps as the day wore on they became romancers, leaving the jousts deserted. When dinner-time came, and they all sat round the table, each in turn put a chapter of his story underneath the potato-bowl—long, endless stories, chapter after chapter diffuse, absorbing, unending, as are the histories of real life; some of these romances were in letters, like *Clarissa Harlowe*. Alfred used to tell a story which lasted for months, and which was called "The Old Horse."

Alfred's first verses, so I once heard him say, were written upon a slate which his brother Charles put into his hand one Sunday at Louth, when all the elders of the party were going into church, and the child was left alone. Charles gave him a subject—the flowers in the garden—and when he came back from church little Alfred brought the slate to his brother all covered with written lines of blank verse. They were made on the model of Thomson's *Seasons*, the only poetry he had ever read. One can picture it all to one's self: the flowers in the garden, the verses, the little poet with waiting eyes, and the young brother scanning the lines. "Yes, you can write," said Charles, and he gave Alfred back the slate.

7

I have also heard another story of his grandfather, later on, asking him to write an elegy on his grandmother, who had recently died, and when it was written, putting ten shillings into his hands and saying, "There, that is the first money you have ever earned by your poetry, and, take my word for it, it will be the last."

The Tennysons are a striking example of the theory of family inheritance. Alfred was one of twelve children, of whom the eldest, Frederick, who was educated at Eton, is known as the author of very imaginative poems. Charles was the second son, and Alfred was the third. Charles and little Alfred were sent for a few years to the Grammar School at Louth, where the Laureate was not happy, although he still remembers walking adorned with blue ribbons in a procession for the proclamation of the coronation of George the Fourth. The old wives said at the time that the boys made the prettiest part of the show.

Charles Tennyson—Charles Turner he was afterwards called, for he took the name with a property which he inherited—was Alfred's special friend and brother. In his own most sweet degree, Charles Tennyson too was a true poet. Who that has ever read his sonnets will cease to love them? His brother loves and quotes them with affection. Coleridge loved them; James Spedding, wise critic, life-long friend, read them with unaltered delight from his youth to his much-honored age. In an introductory essay to a volume of the collected sonnets, published after Charles Turner's death, Mr. Spedding quotes the picture of a summer's day-break:

> "But one sole star, none other anywhere;
> A wild-rose odour from the fields was borne;
> The lark's mysterious joy filled earth and air,
> And from the wind's top met the hunter's horn;
> The aspen trembled wildly; and the morn
> Breathed up in rosy clouds divinely fair."

8

MRS. TENNYSON
After the painting at Aldworth by G. F. Watts, R.A.

Charles Tennyson was in looks not unlike his younger brother. He was stately, too, though shorter in stature, gentle, spiritual, very noble, simple. I once saw him kneeling in a church, and only once again. He was like something out of some other world, more holy, more silent than that in which most of us are living; there is a picture in the National Gallery of St. Jerome which always recalls him to me. The sons must have inherited their poetic gifts from their father. He was the Rev. George Clayton Tennyson, LL.D., a tall, striking, and impressive man, full of accomplishments and parts, a strong nature, high-souled, high-tempered. He was the head of the old family; but his own elder-brother share of its good things had passed by will into the hands of another branch, which is still represented by the Tennysons d'Eyncourt. Perhaps before he died he may have realized that to one of his had come possessions greater than any ever yet entailed by lawyer's deeds—an inheritance, a priceless Benjamin's portion, not to be measured or defined.

II

ALFRED TENNYSON, as he grew up towards manhood, found other and stronger inspirations than Thomson's gentle *Seasons*. Byron's spell had fallen on his generation, and for a boy of genius it must have been absolute and overmastering. Tennyson was soon to find his own voice, but meanwhile he began to write like Byron. He produced poems and verses in endless abundance: trying his wings, as people say, before starting on his own strong flight. One day the news came to the village—the dire news which spread

across the land, filling men's hearts with consternation—
that Byron was dead. Alfred was then a boy about fifteen.

"Byron was dead! I thought the whole world was at an
end," he once said, speaking of these by-gone days. "I
thought everything was over and finished for every one—
that nothing else mattered. I remember I walked out
alone, and carved 'Byron is dead' into the sandstone."

I have spoken of Tennyson from the account of an old
friend, whose recollections go back to those days, which
seem perhaps more distant to us than others of earlier date
and later fashion. Mrs. Tennyson, the mother of the family,
so this same friend tells me, was a sweet and gentle and
most imaginative woman, so kind-hearted that it had passed into a proverb, and the wicked inhabitants of a neighboring village used to bring their dogs to her windows and
beat them in order to be bribed to leave off by the gentle
lady, or to make advantageous bargains by selling her the
worthless curs. She was intensely, fervently religious, as a
poet's mother should be. After her husband's death (he
had added to the rectory, and made it suitable for his large
family) she still lived on at Somersby with her children and
their friends. The daughters were growing up, the elder
sons were going to college. Frederick, the eldest, went first
to Trinity, Cambridge, and his brothers followed him there
in turn. Life was opening for them, they were seeing new
aspects and places, making new friends, and bringing them
home to their Lincolnshire rectory. *In Memoriam* gives
many a glimpse of the old home, of which the echoes still
reach us across half a century.

> "O sound to rout the brood of cares,
>   The sweep of scythe in morning dew,
>   The gust that round the garden flew,
> And tumbled half the mellowing pears!

O bliss, when all in circle drawn
  About him, heart and ear were fed
  To hear him, as he lay and read
The Tuscan poets on the lawn:

Or in the all-golden afternoon
  A guest, or happy sister, sung,
  Or here she brought the harp and flung
A ballad to the brightening moon."

Dean Garden was one of those guests here spoken of, who with Arthur Hallam, the reader of the Tuscan poets, and James Spedding and others, used to gather upon the lawn at Somersby—the young men and women in the light of their youth and high spirits, the widowed mother leading her quiet life within the rectory walls. Was it not a happy sister herself who in after-days once described how, on a lovely summer night, they had all sat up so late talking in the starlight that the dawn came shining unawares; but the young men, instead of going to bed, then and there set off for a long walk across the hills in the sunrise.

"And suck'd from out the distant gloom
  A breeze began to tremble o'er
  The large leaves of the sycamore,*
And fluctuate all the still perfume,

And gathering freshlier overhead,
  Rock'd the full-foliaged elms, and swung
  The heavy-folded rose, and flung
The lilies to and fro, and said

'The dawn, the dawn,' and died away;
  And East and West, without a breath,
  Mixt their dim lights, like life and death,
To broaden into boundless day."

* I am told that the sycamore has been cut down, and the lawn is altered to another shape.

13

III

ONE thing which cannot fail to strike us when we are looking over the records of these earlier days is the remarkable influence which Alfred Tennyson seems to have had from the very first upon his contemporaries, even before his genius had been recognized by the rest of the world. Not only those of his own generation, but his elders and masters seem to have felt something of this. I remember hearing one of Tennyson's oldest friends, Dr. Thompson, the late Master of Trinity, say that "Whewell, who was a man himself, and who knew a man when he saw him," used to pass over in Alfred Tennyson certain informalities and forgetfulness of combinations as to gowns, and places, and times, which in another he would never have overlooked.

Whewell ruled a noble generation—a race of men born in the beginning of the century, whose praise and loyal friendship were indeed worth having, and whose good opinion Tennyson himself may have been proud to possess. Wise, sincere, and witty, these contemporaries spoke with authority, with the moderation of conscious strength. Those of this race that I have known in later days—for they were many of them my father's friends also—have all been men of unmistakable stamp, of great culture, of a certain dignified bearing, and of independence of mind and of nature.

Most of them have succeeded in life as men do who are possessed of intellect and high character. Some have not made the less mark upon their time because their names are less widely known; but each name is a memorable chapter

TENNYSON'S CHILDREN
After the painting at Aldworth by G. F. Watts, R.A.

in life to one and another of us who remember them. One
of those. old friends, who also loved my father, and whom
he loved, who has himself passed away; one who saw life
with his own eyes, and spoke with his own words has described Tennyson in his youth, in a fragment which is a
remembrance, a sort of waking dream, of some by-gone days

and talks. How many of us might have been glad to listen to our poet, and to the poet who has made the philosophy of Omar Khâyâm known to the world, as they discoursed together; of life, of boyish memories, of books, and again more books; of chivalry — mainly but another name for youth—of a possible old age, so thoroughly seasoned with its spirit that all the experience of the world should serve not to freeze but to direct the genial current of the soul! and who that has known them both will not recognize the truth of this description of Alfred in early days?

"A man at all points, of grand proportion and feature, significant of that inward chivalry becoming his ancient and honorable race; when himself a 'Yonge Squire,' like him in *Chaucer*, 'of grete strength,' that could hurl the crowbar farther than any of the neighboring clowns, whose humors, as well as of their betters—knight, squire, landlord, and lieu-tenant—he took quiet note of, like Chaucer himself; like Wordsworth on the mountain, he too when a lad abroad on the world, sometimes of a night with the shepherd, watching not only the flock on the greensward, but also

> 'the fleecy star that bears
> Andromeda far off Atlantic seas,'

along with those other Zodiacal constellations which Aries, I think, leads over the field of heaven."

Arthur Hallam has also written of him in some lines to R. J. Tennant of

> "a friend, a rare one,
> A noble being full of clearest insight,
> . . . whose fame
> Is couching now with pantherized intent,
> As who shall say, I'll spring to him anon,
> And 'have him for my own."

All these men could understand each other, although they had not then told the world their secrets. Poets, critics,

men of learning — such names as Trench and Monckton
Milnes, George Stovin Venables, the Lushingtons and
Kinglake, need no comment; many more there are, and
deans and canons — a band of youthful friends in those days
meeting to hold debate

> "on mind and art,
> And labor, and the changing mart,
> And all the framework of the land;
> When one would aim an arrow fair,
>   But send it slackly from the string;
>   And one would pierce an outer ring,
> And one an inner, here and there;
>
> And last the master-bowman, he,
>   Would cleave the mark."

The lines to J. S. were written to one of these earlier
associates.

> "And gently comes the world to those
>   That are cast in gentle mould."

It was the prophecy of a whole lifetime. There were but few
signs of age in James Spedding's looks, none in his charming companionship, when the accident befell him which took
him away from those who loved him. To another old companion, the Rev. W. H. Brookfield, is dedicated that sonnet
which flows like an echo of Cambridge chimes on a Sabbath
morning.

IV

It is in this sonnet to W. H. Brookfield that Tennyson writes of Arthur Hallam: "Him the lost light of those dawn-golden days."

Arthur Hallam was the same age as my own father, and born in 1811. When he died he was but twenty-three; but he had lived long enough to show what his life might have been.

In the preface to a little volume of his collected poems and essays, published some time after his death, there is a pathetic introduction. "He seemed to tread the earth as a spirit from some better world," writes his father; and a correspondent, who is, as I have been told, Arthur Hallam's and Tennyson's common friend, Mr. Gladstone, says, with deep feeling: "It has pleased God that in his death, as well as in his life and nature, he should be marked beyond ordinary men. When much time has elapsed, when most bereavements will be forgotten, he will still be remembered, and his place, I fear, will be felt to be still vacant; singularly as his mind was calculated by its native tendencies to work powerfully and for good, in an age full of import to the nature and destinies of man."

How completely these words have been carried out must strike us all now. The father lived to see the young man's unconscious influence working through his friend's genius, and reaching whole generations unborn. A lady, speaking of Arthur Hallam after his death, said to Tennyson, "I think he was perfect." "And so he was," said Lord Tennyson,

CLEVEDON COURT

After an unpublished sketch by W. M. Thackeray

"as near perfection as a mortal man can be." Arthur Hallam was a man of remarkable intellect. He could take in the most difficult and abstruse ideas with an extraordinary rapidity and insight. On one occasion he began to work one afternoon, and mastered a difficult book of Descartes at a single sitting. In the preface to the *Memorials* Mr. Hallam speaks of this peculiar clearness of perception and facility for acquiring knowledge; but, above all, the father dwells on his son's undeviating sweetness of disposition and adherence to his sense of what was right. In the Quarterlies and Reviews of the time, his opinion is quoted here and there with a respect which shows in what esteem it was already held.

At the time when Arthur Hallam died he was engaged to be married to a sister of the poet's. She was scarcely seventeen at the time. One of the sonnets addressed by Arthur Hallam to his betrothed was written when he began to teach her Italian:

"Lady, I bid thee to a sunny dome,
    Ringing with echoes of Italian song;
    Henceforth to thee these magic halls belong,
And all the pleasant place is like a home.
Hark, on the right, with full piano tone,
    Old Dante's voice encircles all the air;
    Hark, yet again, like flute-tones mingling rare
Comes the keen sweetness of Petrarca's moan.
Pass thou the lintel freely; without fear
    Feast on the music. I do better know thee
    Than to suspect this pleasure thou dost owe me
Will wrong thy gentle spirit, or make less dear
    That element whence thou must draw thy life—
    An English maiden and an English wife."

As we read the pages of this little book we come upon more than one happy moment saved out of the past, hours of delight and peaceful friendship, saddened by no fore-boding, and complete in themselves.

> "Alfred, I would that you beheld me now,
> Sitting beneath an ivied, mossy wall.
>   . . . Above my head
> Dilates immeasurable a wild of leaves,
> Seeming received into the blue expanse
> That vaults the summer noon."

There is something touching in the tranquil ring of the voice calling out in the summer noontide with all a young man's expansion.

It seemed to be but the beginning of a beautiful happy life, when suddenly the end came. Arthur Hallam was travelling with his father in Austria when he died very suddenly, with scarce a warning sign of illness. Mr. Hallam had come home and found his son, as he supposed, sleeping upon a couch; but it was death, not sleep. "Those whose eyes must long be dim with tears"—so writes the heart-stricken father—"brought him home to rest among his kindred and in his own country." They chose his resting-place in a tranquil spot on a lone hill that overhangs the Bristol Channel. He was buried in the chancel of Clevedon Church, in Somerset, by Clevedon Court, which had been the early home of his mother, an Elton by birth.

In all England there is not a sweeter place than the sunny old Court upon the hill, with its wide prospects and grassy terraces, where Arthur Hallam must have played in his childhood, whence others of his kindred, touched with his own bright and beautiful spirit, have come forth.

When Mr. Hallam, after a life of repeated sorrows, at last went to his rest with his wife and his children, it was Alfred Tennyson who wrote his epitaph, which may still be read in the chancel of the old Clevedon Church.

V

ONCE in their early youth we hear of the two friends, Tennyson and Hallam, travelling in the Pyrenees. This was at the time of the war of Spanish independence, when many generous young men went over with funds and good energies to help the cause of liberty. These two were taking money and letters written in invisible ink to certain conspirators who were then revolting against the intolerable tyranny of Ferdinand, and who were chiefly hiding in the Pyrenees. The young men met, among others, a Señor Ojeda, who confided to Tennyson his intentions, which were to *couper la gorge à tous les curés*. Señor Ojeda could not talk English or fully explain all his aspirations. "*Mais vous connaissez mon cœur,*" said he, effusively: and a pretty black one it is, thought the poet. I have heard Tennyson described in those days as "straight and with a broad breast," and when he had crossed over from the Continent and was coming back, walking through Wales, he went one day into a little way-side inn, where an old man sat by the fire, who looked up, and asked many questions. "Are you from the army? Not from the army? Then where do you come from?" said the old man. "I am just come from the Pyrenees," said Alfred. "Ah, I knew there was a something," said the wise old man.

John Kemble was among those who had gone over to Spain, and one day a rumor came to distant Somersby that he was to be tried for his life by the Spanish authorities. No one else knew much about him except Alfred Tennyson, who

THE MEETING OF THE SEVERN AND WYE.

started before dawn to drive across the country in search of
some person of authority who knew the Consul at Cadiz, and
who could send letters of protection to the poor prisoner.

It was a false alarm. John Kemble came home to make
a name for himself in other fields. Meanwhile Alfred Ten-

nyson's own reputation was growing, and when the first two volumes of his collected poems were published in 1842, followed by *The Princess*, in 1847, his fame spread throughout the land.

Some of the reviews were violent and antagonistic at first. One especially had tasted blood, and the " Hang. draw, and *Quarterly*," as it has been called, of those days, having lately cut up *Endymion*, now proceeded to demolish Tennyson.

But this was a passing phase. It is curious to note the sudden change in the tone of the criticisms — the absolute surrender of these knights of the pen to the irresistible and brilliant advance of the unknown and visored warrior. The visor is raised now, the face is familiar to us all, and the arms, though tested in a hundred fights, are shining and unconquered still.

William Howitt, whom we have already quoted, has written an article upon the Tennyson of these earlier days. It is fanciful, suggestive, full of interest, with a gentle mysterious play and tender appreciation. Speaking of the poet himself, he asks, with the rest of the world at that time : " You may hear his voice, but where is the man? He is wandering in some dream-land, beneath the shade of old and charmed forests, by far-off shores, where

> . 'all night
> The plunging seas draw backward from the land
> Their moon-led waters white ;

by the old mill-dam, thinking of the merry miller and his pretty daughter ; or wandering over the open wolds where

> ' Norland whirlwinds blow.'

From all these places—from the silent corridor of an ancient convent, from some shrine where a devoted knight recites his vows, from the drear monotony of 'the moated grange,' or the forest beneath the 'talking oak'—comes the voice of Tennyson, rich, dreamy, passionate, yet not impatient, musical with the airs of chivalrous ages, yet mingling in his song the theme and the spirit of those that are yet to come." . . .

This article was written many years ago, when but the first chords had sounded, before the glorious Muse, passing beyond her morning joy, had met with the sorrow of life. But it is well that as we travel on through later, sadder scenes we should still carry in our hearts this romantic music. One must be English born, I think, to know how English is the spell which this great enchanter casts over us; the very spirit of the land falls upon us as the visions he evokes come closing round. Whether it is the moated grange he shows us, or Locksley Hall that in the distance overlooks the sandy tracts, or Dora standing in the corn, or the sight of the brimming wave that swings through quiet meadows round the mill, it is all home in its broadest, sweetest aspect.

It would not be easy for a generation that has grown up to the music of Tennyson, that has in a manner beaten time to it with the pulse of its life, to imagine what the world would be without it. Even the most original among us must needs think of things more or less in the shape in which they come before us. The mystery of the charm of words is as great as that by which a wonder of natural beauty comes around us, and lays hold of our imagination. It may be fancy, but I for one feel as if summer-time could scarcely be summer without the song of the familiar green books.

CAERLEON UPON USK.

VI

In Memoriam, with music in its cantos, belonging to the school of all men's sad hearts, rings the awful *De Profundis* of death, faced and realized as far as may be by a human soul. It came striking suddenly into all the sweet ideal beauty and lovely wealth which had gone before, with a revelation of that secret of life which is told to each of us in turn by the sorrow of its own soul. Nothing can be more simple than the form of the poem as it flows.

> "Short swallow-flights of song, that dip
>   Their wings in tears, and skim away,"

as the poet says himself, but it is something else besides—something which has given words and ease to many of those who in their lonely frozen grief perhaps feel that they are no longer quite alone, when such a voice as this can reach them :

> "Peace ; come away : the song of woe
>   Is after all an earthly song :
>   Peace ; come away : we do him wrong
>   To sing so wildly : let us go."

And as the cry passes away, come signs of peace and dawning light.:

> "Be neither song, nor game, nor feast ;
>   Nor harp be touch'd, nor flute be blown ;
>   No dance, no motion, save alone
>   What lightens in the lucid east

29

"Of rising worlds by yonder wood.
   Long sleeps the summer in the seed;
   Run out your measured arcs, and lead
  The closing cycle rich in good."

And the teacher who can read the great book of nature interprets for us as he turns the page.

With *In Memoriam*, which was not published till 1850, Alfred Tennyson's fame was firmly established; and when

BURLEIGH HOUSE, BY STAMFORD TOWN

Wordsworth died (on Shakespeare's day in that same year) its author was appointed by the Queen Poet Laureate. There is a story* that at the time Sir Robert Peel was consulted he had never read any Tennyson, but he read "Ulysses" and warmed up, and acknowledged the right of this new-come poet to be England's Laureate.

The home at Somersby was broken up by this time, by

* See Lord Houghton's Memoirs.

marriages and other family events. Alfred Tennyson had come to live in London. He was poor; he had in turn to meet that struggle with wholesome poverty which brings the vagueness of genius into contact with reality, and teaches, better, perhaps, than any other science, the patience, the forbearance, and knowledge of life which belong to it.

The Princess, with all her lovely court and glowing harmonies, had been born in London, among the fogs and smuts of Lincoln's Inn, although, like all works of true art, this poem must have grown by degrees in other times and places as the poet came and went, free, unshackled, meditating, inditing. He says that "Tears, Idle Tears," was suggested by Tintern Abbey: but who shall define by what mysterious wonder of beauty and regret, by what sense of the "transient with the abiding?"

In Memoriam was followed by the first part of the *Idylls*, and the record of the court King Arthur held at Camelot, and at "old Caerleon upon Usk" on that eventful Whitsuntide when Prince Geraint came quickly flashing through the shallow ford to the little knoll, where the queen stood with her maiden, and

> . . . "listen'd for the distant hunt,
> And chiefly for the baying of Cavall."

If *In Memoriam* is the record of a human soul, the *Idylls* mean the history, not of one man or of one generation, but of a whole cycle, of the faith of a nation failing and falling away into darkness. The first "Idyll" and the last, I have heard Lord Tennyson say, are intentionally more archaic than the others. "The whole is the dream of man coming into practical life, and ruined by one sin." Birth is a mystery, and death is a mystery, and in the midst lies the tableland of life, and its struggle and performance.

The poet once told us that the song of the knights marching past the King at the marriage of Arthur was made one spring afternoon on Clapham Common as he walked along.

> "Blow trumpet, for the world is white with May;
> Blow trumpet, the long night hath roll'd away!
> Blow through the living world—'Let the King reign.'"

So sang the young knights in the first bright days of early chivalry.

> "Clang battle-axe, and clash brand! Let the King reign.
> The King will follow Christ, and we the King."

And then when the doom of evil spread, bringing not sorrow alone, but destruction in its train, not death only, but hopelessness and consternation, the song is finally changed into an echo of strange woe; we hear no shout of triumph, but the dim shocks of battle,

> "the crash
> Of battle-axe on shatter'd helms, and shrieks
> After the Christ, of those who falling down
> Look'd up for heaven, and only saw the mist."

All is over with the fair court; Guinevere's golden head is low; she has fled to Almesbury—

> "Fled all night long by glimmering waste and weald,
> And heard the Spirits of the waste and weald
> Moan as she fled, or thought she heard them moan:
> And in herself she moan'd, 'Too late, too late!'
> Till in the cold wind that foreruns the morn,
> A blot in heaven, the Raven, flying high,
> Croak'd, and she thought, 'He spies a field of death.'"

And finally comes the conclusion, and the "Passing of Arthur," and he vanishes as he came, in mystery, silently floating away upon the barge towards the East, whence all religions are said to come.

ALMESBURY

As the writer notes down these various fragments of re-membrance, and compiles this sketch of present things, she cannot but feel how much of the past it all means to her, and how very much her own feeling is an inheritance which has gathered interest during a lifetime, so that the chief claim of her words to be regarded is that they are those of an old friend. Her father's warmth of admiration comes back vividly as she writes, all his pleasure when he secured "Tithonus" for one of the early numbers of the ' *Cornhill Magazine,* his immense and outspoken admiration for the *Idylls of the King.*

I have heard them all speak of these London days when Alfred Tennyson lived in poverty with his friends and his golden dreams. He lived in the Temple, at 58 Lincoln's Inn Fields, and elsewhere.

It was about this time that Carlyle introduced Sir John Simeon to Tennyson one night at Bath House, and made the often-quoted speech, "There he sits upon a dung-heap surrounded by innumerable dead dogs;" by which dead dogs he meant "Œnone" and other Greek versions and adaptations. He had said the same thing of Landor and his Hellenics. "I was told of this," said Lord Tennyson, "and some time afterwards I repeated it to Carlyle: 'I'm told that is what you say of me.' He gave a kind of guf-faw. 'Eh, that wasn't a very luminous description of you,' he answered."

The story is well worth retelling, so completely does it illustrate the grim humor and unaffected candor of a dys-peptic man of genius, who flung words and epithets without malice, who neither realized the pain his chance sallies might give, nor the indelible flash which branded them upon people's memories.

The world has pointed its moral finger of late at the old man in his great old age, accusing himself in the face of all, and confessing the overpowering irritations which the suffering of a lifetime had laid upon him and upon her he loved. That old caustic man of deepest feeling, with an ill temper and a tender heart and a racking imagination, speaking from the grave, and bearing unto it that cross of passionate remorse which few among us dare to face, seems to some of us now a figure nobler and truer, a teacher greater far, than in the days when his pain and love and remorse were still hidden from us all.

Carlyle and Mr. Fitzgerald used to be often with Tennyson at that time. They used to dine together at the "Cock" tavern in the Strand among other places; sometimes Tennyson and Carlyle took long, solitary walks into the night.

Here is Carlyle's description of the poet, written to Emerson in America:

"Tennyson came in to us on Sunday evening, a truly interesting Son of Earth and Son of Heaven. . . . One of the finest-looking men in the world. His voice is musical, metallic—fit for loud laughter and piercing wail, and all that may be between; speech and speculation free and plenteous. I do not meet in these late decades such company over a pipe. . . . A true human soul or some authentic approximation thereto, to whom your soul can say, Brother; a man solitary and sad as certain men are, dwelling in an atmosphere of gloom—carrying *a bit of chaos about him, in short, which he is manufacturing into cosmos!*" I have ventured to put the italics; had I letters of gold to write with I would set them to the stately words.

The other day a lady was describing a by-gone feast given about this time by the poet to Lady Duff Gordon, and to another young and beautiful lady, a niece of Mr. Hallam's. Harry Hallam, his younger son, was also asked. Lord Tennyson, in his hospitality, had sent for a carpenter to change the whole furniture of his bedroom in order to prepare a

FARRINGFORD HOUSE, ISLE OF WIGHT
From a photograph by Perkins & Son, London

proper drawing-room for the ladies. Mr. Brookfield, coming in, was in time to suggest some compromise, to which the host reluctantly agreed. One can imagine that it was a delightful feast, but indeed it is always a feast-day when one breaks bread with those one loves, and the writer is glad to think that she, too, has been among those to sit at the kind board where the salt has not lost its savor in the years that have passed, and where the guests can say their grace not for bread and wine alone. May she add that the first occasion of her having the honor of breaking bread in company with Lord Tennyson was in her father's house, when she was propped up in a tall chair between her parents?

VII

Some of the writer's earliest recollections are of days now long gone by, when many of these young men of whom she has been speaking, grown to be middle-aged, used to come from time to time to her father's house, and smoke with him, and talk and laugh quietly, taking life seriously, but humorously too, with a certain loyalty to others and self-respect which was their characteristic. They were somewhat melancholy men at soul; but for that very reason, perhaps, the humors of life may have struck them more especially. It is no less possible that our children will think of us as cheerful folks upon the whole, with no little affectation of melancholy and all the graces.

I can remember on one occasion through a cloud of smoke looking across a darkening room at the noble, grave head of the Poet Laureate. He was sitting with my father in the twilight after some family meal in the old house in

Kensington. It is Lord Tennyson himself who has reminded me how upon this occasion, while my father was
speaking, my little sister looked up suddenly from the book
over which she had been absorbed, saying, in her sweet
childish voice, "Papa, why do you not write books like
Nicholas Nickleby?" Then again I seem to hear, across
that same familiar table, voices without shape or name,
talking and telling each other that Lord Tennyson was married—that he and his wife had been met walking on the
terrace at Clevedon Court; and then the clouds descend
again, except, indeed, that I still see my father riding off
on his brown cob to the Tennysons' house at Twickenham
(Chapel House, which I can remember with its oak staircase
and the carved figure of a bishop blessing the passers-by)
to attend the christening of Hallam, their eldest son. In
after-days we were shown the old ivy-grown church and
the rectory at Shiplake, by the deep bend of the Thames,
where their marriage took place, after long years of faithful
constancy.

It was at Somersby that Alfred Tennyson first became
acquainted with his wife. She was eldest daughter of
Henry Selwood, the last but one of a family of country
gentlemen settled in Berkshire in the time of Charles I.,
and before that, in Saxon times, as it is said, more important people in the forest of their name. Her mother was a
sister of Sir John Franklin.

Not many years after their marriage Mr. and Mrs. Tennyson settled at Freshwater, in the Isle of Wight. There is
a photograph I have always liked, in which it seems to me
the history of this home is written, as such histories should
be written, in sunlight, in the flashing of a beam, in an
instant, and forever. It was taken in the green glade at
Farringford. Hallam and Lionel Tennyson stand on either
side of their parents, the father and mother and children,

IN THE NEW FOREST

hand in hand, come advancing towards us—who does not
know the beautiful lines to the mother :

> "Dear, near, and true—no truer Time himself
> Can prove you, though he make you evermore
> Dearer and nearer."

And though years have passed in which the boys with
their wind-blown locks grew up to man's estate, so that it
is now their boys who are in turn picking the daffodils under
the Farringford hedge, yet the old picture remains, in which
that one dear remembered figure, so early carried by the
flood far "from out our bourne of Time and Space," seems
to shine brighter than the rest.

VIII

ONE autumn, when everything seemed happy at home,
Mrs. Cameron took me with her to Freshwater for a few delightful weeks, and then, for the first time, I lived with them
all, and with kind Mrs. Cameron, in the ivy-grown house
near the gates of Farringford. For the first time I stayed
in the island, and with the people who were dwelling there,
and walked with Tennyson along High Down, treading the
turf, listening to his talk, while the gulls came sideways,
flashing their white breasts against the edge of the cliffs, and
the poet's cloak flapped time to the gusts of the west wind.
The house at Farringford itself seemed like a charmed
palace, with green walls without, and speaking walls within.
There hung Dante with his solemn nose and wreath ; Italy
gleamed over the doorways ; friends' faces lined the pas-

sages; books filled the shelves, and a glow of crimson was everywhere; the great oriel drawing-room window was full of green and golden leaves, of the sound of birds and of the distant sea.

The very names of the people who have stood upon the lawn at Farringford would be an interesting study for some future biographer : Longfellow, Maurice, Kingsley, the Duke of Argyll, Locker, Dean Stanley, the Prince Consort. Good Garibaldi once planted a tree there, off which some too ardent republican broke a branch before twenty-four hours had passed. Here came Clough in the last year of his life. Here Mrs. Cameron fixed her lens, marking the well-known faces as they passed : Darwin and Henry Taylor, Watts and Aubrey de Vere, Lecky and Jowett, and a score of others.

I first knew the place in the autumn, but perhaps it is even more beautiful in the spring-time, when all day the lark trills high overhead, and then when the lark has flown out of hearing the thrushes begin, and the air is sweet with scents from the many fragrant shrubs. The woods are full of anemones and primroses; narcissus grows wild in the lower fields; a lovely creamy stream of flowers flows along the lanes, and lies hidden in the levels; hyacinth pools of blue shine in the woods; and then with a later burst of glory comes the gorse, lighting up the country round about, and blazing on the beacon hill. The little sketch here given was made early one morning by Frederick Walker, who had come over to see us at Freshwater. The beacon hill stands behind Farringford. If you cross the little wood of nightingales and thrushes, and follow the lane where the blackthorn hedges shine (lovely dials that illuminate to show the hour), you come to the downs, and climbing their smooth steeps you reach "High Down," where the beacon-staff stands firm upon the mound. Then, following the line of the cliffs, you come at last to the Needles, and may look

I hate the dreadful hollow behind the little wood

TENNYSON READING "MAUD"

From a sketch by Dante Gabriel Rossetti, 1855. [See Note on page 60.]

down upon the ridge of rocks that rise, crisp, sharp, shining, out of the blue wash of fierce, delicious waters.

The lovely places and sweet country all about Farringford are not among the least of its charms. Beyond the Primrose Island itself and the blue Solent, the New Forest spreads its shades, and the green depths reach to the very shores. Have we not all read of the forest where Merlin was becharmed, where the winds were still in the wild

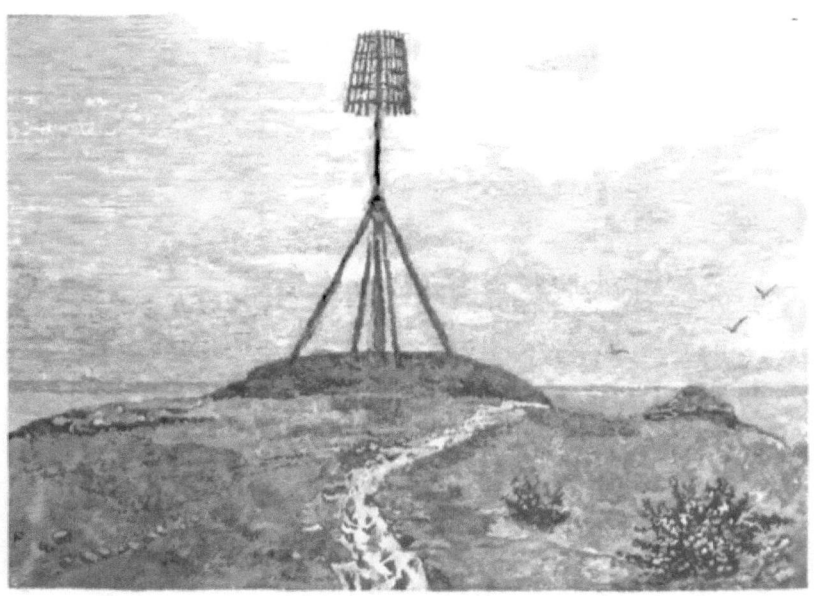

FARRINGFORD BEACON
From an unpublished sketch by Frederick Walker

woods of Broceliande? The forest of Brockenhurst, in Hampshire, waves no less green, its ferns and depths are no less sweet and sylvan, than those of Brittany.

> "Before an oak, so hollow, huge, and old
> It look'd a tower of ruin'd mason-work,
> At Merlin's feet the wily Vivien lay."

Some people camping in the New Forest once told me of a mysterious figure in a cloak coming suddenly upon them out of a deep glade, passing straight on, looking neither to the right nor the left. "It was either a ghost or it was Mr. Tennyson," said they.

In Sir John Simeon's lifetime there was a constant intercourse between Farringford and Swanston. Sir John was one of Tennyson's most constant companions—a knight of courtesy he calls him in the sad lines written in the garden at Swanston.

Maud grew out of a remark of Sir John Simeon's, to whom Tennyson had read the lines,

> "O that 'twere possible
> After long grief and pain,"

which lines were, so to speak, the heart of *Maud*. Sir John said that it seemed to him as if something were wanting to explain the story of this poem, and so by degrees it all grew. One little story was told me on the authority of Mr. Henry Sidgwick, who was perhaps present on that occasion. Tennyson was reading the poem to a silent company assembled in the twilight, and when he came to the birds in the high hall garden calling Maud, Maud, Maud, Maud, he stopped short, and asked an authoress who happened to be present what birds these were. The authoress, much alarmed, and feeling that she must speak, and that the eyes of the whole company were upon her, faltered out, "Nightingales." "Pooh," said Tennyson, "what a cockney you are! Nightingales don't say Maud. Rooks do, or something like it. Caw, caw, caw, caw, caw." Then he went on reading.

Reading, is it? One can hardly describe it. It is a sort of mystical incantation, a chant in which every note rises and falls and reverberates again. As we sit around the

THE OAK LAWN, ALDWORTH

twilight room at Farringford, with its great oriel-window looking to the garden, across fields of hyacinth and self-sowed daffodils towards the sea, where the waves wash against the rock, we seem carried by a tide not unlike the ocean's sound; it fills the room, it ebbs and flows away; and when we leave, it is with a strange music in our ears, feeling that we have for the first time, perhaps, heard what we may have read a hundred times before.

Let me here note a fact, whether a tort or apropos of nightingales: once when Mr. Tennyson was in Yorkshire, so he told me, as he was walking at night in a friend's garden, he heard a nightingale singing with such a frenzy of passion that it was unconscious of everything else, and not frightened though he came and stood quite close beside it; he could see its eye flashing, and feel the air bubble in his ear through the vibration. Our poet, with his short-sighted eyes, can see farther than most people. Almost the first time I ever walked out with him, he told me to look and tell him if the field-lark did not come down sideways upon its wing.

Nature in its various aspects makes up a larger part of this man's life than it does for other people. He goes his way unconsciously absorbing life, and its lights and sounds, and teaching us to do the same as far as may be. There is an instance of this given in the pamphlet already quoted from, where the two friends talk on of one theme and another from Kenelm Digby to Aristophanes, and the poet is described as saying, among other things, that he knows of no human outlook so solemn as that from an infant's eyes, and that it was from those of his own he learned that those of the Divine Child in Raffaello's Sistine Madonna were not overcharged with expression.

Here is a reminiscence of Tennyson's about the echo at Killarney, where he said to the boatman, "When I last was here I heard eight echoes, and now I only hear one." To which the man, who had heard people quoting the bugle song, replied, "Why, you must be the gentleman that brought all the money to the place."

People have different ideas of poets. Mrs. B——, of Totland's Bay, once asked a Freshwater boy, who was driving her, "if he knew Mr. Tennyson." "He makes poets for the Queen," said the boy. "What do you mean?" said the lady, amused. "I don't know what they means," said the boy, "but p'liceman often seen him walking about a-making of 'em under the stars." The author of *Euphranor* has his own definition of a poet:

"The only living—and like to live—poet I have known, when he found himself beside the 'bonnie Doon,' whether it were from recollection of poor Burns, or of 'the days that are no more' which haunt us all, I know not—I think he did not know—'broke into a passion of tears' (as he told me). Of tears, which during a pretty long and intimate intercourse I had never seen glistening in his eyes but once, when reading Virgil—'dear old Virgil,' as he called him—together; and then —oh, not of Queen Dido, nor of young Marcellus even, but of the burning of Troy, in the second Æneid—whether moved by the catastrophe itself, or the majesty of the verse it is told in, or as before, scarce knowing why. For as King Arthur shall bear witness, no young Edwin he, though, as a great poet, comprehending all the softer stops of human emotion in that diapason where the intellectual, no less than what is called the poetical, faculty predominated."

"You will last," Douglas Jerrold said. And there was Carlyle's "Eh! he has got the grip of it," when Tennyson read him the *Revenge*. But perhaps the best compliment Mr. Tennyson ever received was one day when walking in Covent Garden, when he was stopped by a rough-looking man, who held out his hand, and said: "You're Mr. Tennyson. Look here, sir, here am I. I've been drunk for six days out of the seven, but if you will shake me by the hand, I'm d——d if I ever get drunk again."

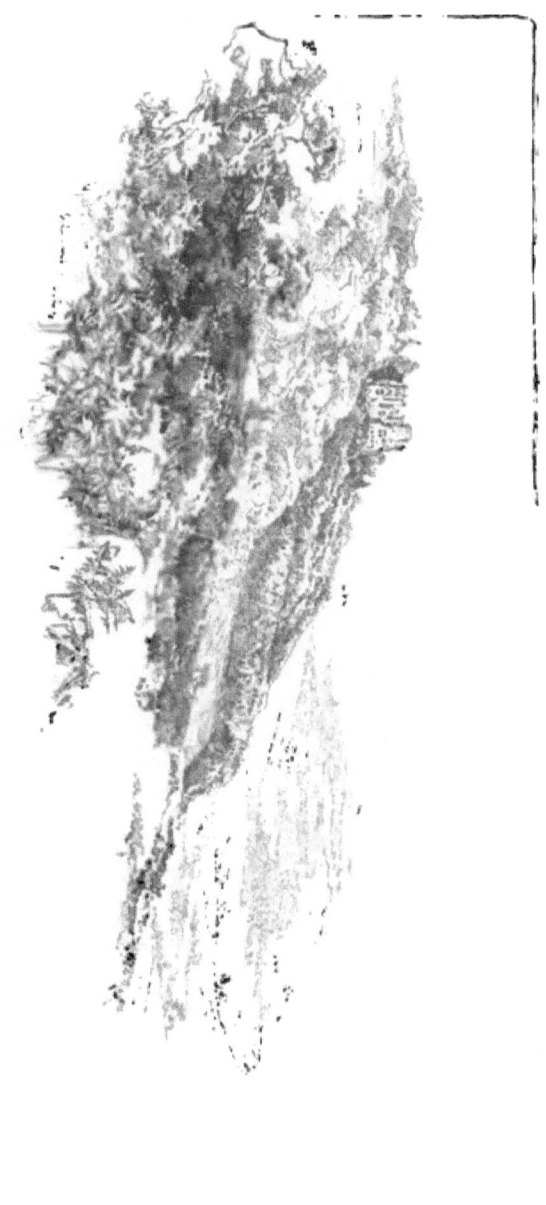

THE EDGE OF BLACKDOWN, SHOWING TENNYSON'S HOUSE

IX

ALDWORTH was built some twenty years ago, when Lady Tennyson had been ordered change, and Freshwater was found to be unbearable and overcrowded during the summer months. It must be borne in mind that to hospitable people there are dangers from friendly inroads as well as from the attacks of enemies. The new house, where for many years past the family has spent its summers, stands on the summit of a high, lonely hill in Surrey, and yet it is not quite out of reach of London life. It is a white stone house with many broad windows facing a great view and a long terrace, like some one of those at Siena or Perugia, with a low parapet of stone, where ivies and roses are trained, making a foreground to the lovely haze of the distance. Sometimes at Aldworth, when the summer days are at their brightest, and Blackdown top has been well warmed and sunned, I have seen a little procession coming along the terrace walk, and proceeding by its green boundary into a garden, where the sun shines its hottest, upon a sheltered lawn, and where standard rose-trees burn their flames: Lord Tennyson, in his cloak, going first, perhaps dragging the garden chair in which Lady Tennyson was lying: Hallam Tennyson following, with rugs and cushions for the rest of the party. If the little grandsons and their mother, in her white dress and broad, shady hat, and Lionel Tennyson's boys, absorbed in their books of adventure, are there, the family group is complete. One special day I remember when we all sat for an hour round about the homely chair and its gentle occupant. It seemed not unlike a realization of some Italian picture that I had somewhere seen: the tranquil eyes, the peaceful heights, the glorious summer day, some sense of lasting calm, of beauty beyond the present hour.

Lord Tennyson works alone in the early hours of the morning, and comes down long after his own frugal meal is over to find his guests assembling round the social breakfast-table. He generally goes out for a walk before luncheon, with his son and a friend, perhaps, and followed by a couple of dogs. Most of us know the look of the stately figure, the hanging cloak, and broad felt hat.

There used to be one little ceremony peculiar to the Tennyson family, and reminding one of some college custom which continued, that when dinner was over the guests used to be brought away into a second room, where stood a white table, upon which fruit and wine were set, and a fire burned bright, and a pleasant hour went by, while the master of the house sat in his carved chair and discoursed upon any topic suggested by his guests, or brought forth reminiscences of early Lincolnshire days, or from facts remembered out of the lives of past men who have been his friends. There was Rogers, among the rest, for whom he had a great affection, with whom he constantly lived during that lonely time in London. "I have dined alone with him," I heard Lord Tennyson say, "and we have talked about death till the tears rolled down his face."

Tennyson met Tom Moore at Rogers's, and there, too, he first met Mr. Gladstone. John Forster, Leigh Hunt, and Landor were also friends of that time. One of Tennyson's often companions in those days was Mr. Hallam, whose opinion he once asked of Carlyle's *French Revolution*. Mr. Hallam replied, in his quick, rapid way, "Upon my

TENNYSON'S HOME AT ALDWORTH, SURREY

word, I once opened the book, and read four or five pages. The style is so abominable I could not get on with it." Whereas Carlyle's own criticism upon the *History of the Middle Ages* was, "Eh! the poor, miserable skeleton of a book!"

Was it not Charles Lamb who wanted to return grace after reading Shakespeare, little deeming in humble simplicity that many of us yet to come would be glad to return thanks for a jest of Charles Lamb's. The difference between those who speak with reality, and those who go through life fitting their second-hand ideas to other people's words, is one so marked that even a child may tell the difference. When the Laureate speaks, every word comes wise, racy, absolutely natural, and sincere : and how gladly do we listen to his delightful stories, full of odd humors and knowledge of men and women, or to his graver talk! I remember thinking how true was the phrase of Lionel Tennyson's concerning his father, "When a man has read so much and thought so much, it is an epitome of the knowledge of to-day we find in him," an epitome indeed touched by the solemn strain of the poet's own gift. I once heard Tennyson talking to some actors, to no less a person indeed than to Hamlet himself, for after the curtain fell the whole play seemed to flow from off the stage into the box where we had been sitting, and I could scarcely tell at last where reality began and Shakespeare ended. The play was over, and we ourselves seemed a part of it still; here were the players, and our own prince poet, in that familiar simple voice we all know, explaining the art, going straight to the point in his own downright fashion, criticising with delicate appreciation, by the simple force of truth and conviction carrying all before him. "You are a good actor lost," one of these, the real actor, said to him.

It is a gain to the world when people are content to be

themselves, not chipped to the smooth pattern of the times, but simple, original, and unaffected in ways and words. Here is a poet leading a poet's life; where he goes there goes the spirit of his home, whether in London among the crowds, or at Aldworth on the lonely height, or at Farringford in that beautiful bay. The last time I went to see him in London he was smoking in a top room in Eton Square. It may interest an American public to be told that it was Durham tobacco from North Carolina, which Mr. Lowell had given him. I could not but feel how little even circumstance itself can contribute to that mysterious essence of individuality which we all recognize and love. In this commonplace London room, with all the stucco of Belgravia round about, I found the old dream realized, the old charm of youthful impression. There sat my friend as I had first seen him years ago among the clouds.

NOTE.—This early sketch was preserved by Robert Browning, to whose courtesy we are indebted for its use, and was one of the interesting pictures of the Rossetti exhibition held in London after the painter's death. Mrs. Browning was another of the distinguished company.

THE TENNYSON COAT OF ARMS

JOHN RUSKIN

" Let knowledge grow from more to more,
But more of reverence in us dwell ;
That mind and soul, according well,
May make one music as before."

BRANTWOOD

I

WHEN the writer of this essay tries to go back to her first impressions of John Ruskin, she finds that they must date from the round-table in the middle of her father's drawing-room in Kensington — the little drawing-room in Young

Street, with the bow-windows, the oak-leaved carpet, the polished bookcase with its glass doors, and the aforesaid round-table with its dial of books arranged in a circle, and faithfully marking the march of time. For, looking at a list of Mr. Ruskin's works, I find that the *Seven Lamps of Architecture* was published in 1849, soon after we came to live in England in our father's house. And in this year there appeared among the *Punches* and the lovely red silk Annuals and Keepsakes that illuminated the bow-windowed room a volume bound (so it seemed to us children) in moulded slabs of pure chocolate. I can still recall the look of the broad margins, the pictures, and noble-looking printed pages, and although the Annuals with the fascinating brides and veiled ladies, and the ghosts and guitars and brigands, were perhaps more to our childish tastes, even then we realized in some indefinite way the importance of the big brown book which opened like a casket, and gathered some impressions of palace windows and of carved shadows from its pages—impressions to be afterwards turned into actual stone and sunlight.

As time went on, the *Stones of Venice* in due course took their place upon our dial, and meanwhile the name of the writer of the beautiful authoritative books is among those other echoes, which are so familiar that one can scarcely tell when they begin to sound.

In the first page of the eleventh chapter of *Præterita* occurs the name of "Mrs. John Simon, who," says Ruskin, "in my mother's old age was her most deeply trusted friend." It was at this lady's house, sitting by the kind hostess of many a year to be, that the writer first saw the author of *Modern Painters*, while at the other end of the table Mr. Simon, now Sir John ("Brother John," Ruskin dubbed him long since), sat carving, as was his wont, roast mutton—"be it tender and smoking and juicy"—and dispensing, as is still his wont, trimmings and oracles and epigrams with every plateful.

I could even now quote some of the words Ruskin spoke on that summer's evening in Great Cumberland Street, and I can see him as he was then almost as plainly as on the last time that we met. His mood on that first occasion was one of deep depression, and I can remember being frightened as well as absorbed by his talk. Was he joking? was he serious? I could hardly follow what he said then, though now it all seems simple enough. But good company is like good wine, and improves by keeping, and let us hope that this applies to the recipients as well as to the feast itself.

Ruskin seemed less picturesque as a young man than in his later days. Perhaps gray waving hair may be more becoming than darker locks, but the speaking, earnest eyes must have been the same, as well as the tones of that delightful voice, with its slightly foreign pronunciation of the *r*, which seemed so familiar again when it welcomed us to Coniston long, long years after. Meeting thus after fifteen years, I was struck by the change for the better in him; by the bright, radiant, sylvan look which a man gains by living among woods and hills and pure breezes.

THE road to Brantwood * runs beneath the old trees which shade the head of Coniston Water, and you leave the village and the inn behind, and the Thwaite, with its pretty old gardens and peacocks, and skirt the beautiful grounds of Monk Coniston; you pass the ivy tower where the lords of the manor keep their boats; and the reeds among which the swallows and dragon-flies are darting; and as you advance, if you look back across the green hay-fields and wooded slopes of Monk Coniston, you can see Weatherlam and Ravenscrag, with Yewdale for a back-ground, while Coniston Old Man on the opposite side of the lake rises like a Pilatus above the village, and soars into changing lights and clouds. Then, as you walk still farther along the road, leaving all these things behind, you pass into a sweet Arcadia, in which, indeed, one loses one's self again in after-times. You go by Tent Lodge, where Tennyson once dwelt, where the beautiful Romneys are hanging on the walls; you pass the cottage with roses for bricks, and with jasmines and honeysuckles for thatch, and the farm where the pet lamb used to dwell, to the terror of the children (it seemed appropriate enough to Wordsworth's

---

* Ruskin, writing of his earliest recollections of Coniston in *Præterita*, says: "The inn at Coniston was then actually at the upper end of the lake, the road from Amble-side to the village passing just between it and the water, and the view of the long reach of lake, with its softly wooded lateral hills, had for my father a tender charm which ex-cited the same feeling as that with which he afterwards regarded the lakes of Italy. Lowwood Inn also was then little more than a country cottage, and Ambleside a rural village, and the absolute peace and bliss which any one who cared for grassy hills and for sweet waters might find at every footstep and at every turn of crag or bend of bog was totally unlike anything I ever saw or read of elsewhere."

country, but I can remember a little baby girl wild with terror and flying from its gambols); then, still following the road, you reach a delightful cackling colony of poultry and ducks, where certain hospitable ladies used to experimentalize, and prove to us whether or no eggs are eggs (as these ladies have determined eggs should be); then comes Low Bank Ground, our own little farm lodging among the chestnut-trees and meadows full of flowers. It had been the site of a priory once, and on this slope and in the shade of the chestnut-trees, where monks once dwelt, the writer met Ruskin again after many years. He, the master of Brantwood, came, as I remember, dressed with some ceremony, meeting us with a certain old-fashioned courtesy and manner; but he spoke with his heart, of which the fashion doesn't change happily from one decade to another; and as he stood in his tall hat and frock-coat upon the green, the clouds and drifts came blowing up from every quarter of heaven, and I can almost see him while he talked with emphasis and remembrance of that which was then in both our minds. Low Bank Ground is but a very little way from Brantwood; you can go there by land or by water. If you walk, the road climbs the spur of the hill, and runs below moors by a wood where squirrels sit under the oak-trees and honeysuckles drop from the branches; or, if you like to go by the lake, you can get Timothy from the farm to row you. "A dash of the oars, and you are there," as Ruskin said, and accordingly we started in the old punt for our return visit to Brantwood.

The sun came out between rain clouds as the boat struck with a hollow crunch against the stones of the tiny landing pier. Timothy from the farm, who had come to pilot us, told us with a sympathetic grin that Mr. Ruskin—"Rooskin," I think he called him—"had built t' pier, and set t' stoans himsel' wi' the other gentlemen, but they had to send for t' smith from the village to make t' bolts faaster." The pier is fast enough, running out into the lake, with a little fleet safely anchored behind it, while Brantwood stands high up on the slope, with square windows looking across the waters. Just on the other side of the lake, wrapped in mysterious ivy wreaths, where the cows are whisking their tails beneath the elms, rise the gables of the old farm, once the manor-house where "Sidney's sister, Pembroke's mother," once dwelt. Sir Philip Sidney used to come riding across the distant hills to visit her there—so tradition says. The mere thought of Coniston Water brings back the peaceful legends and sounds all about Ruskin's home : the plash of the lake, the rustle of the leaves and rushes, the beat of birds on their whirring wings, the flop of the water-rats, the many buzzing and splashing and delicious things. A path up a garden of fruit and flowers, of carnations and straw-berries, leads with gay zigzags to the lawn in front of the Brantwood windows.

The house is white, plain, and comfortable, absolutely unpretending. I remember noticing, with a thrill, the umbrella-stand in the glass door. So Mr. Ruskin had an umbrella just like other people ! It seemed to me to be a dwelling planned for sunshine, and sunshine on the lakes is of a quality so sweet and rare that it counts for more than in any other place. The brightness of Brantwood, the squareness, and its unaffected comfortableness, were, I think, the chief characteristics. You had a general impression of solid, old-fashioned furniture, of amber-colored damask curtains and coverings ; there were Turners and other water-color pictures in curly frames upon the drawing-room walls — a Prout, I think, among them ; there was a noble Titian in the dining-room, and the full-length portrait of a child in a blue sash over the sideboard, which has become familiar since then to the readers of *Præterita;* and

most certainly was there an absence of any of the art-diph-
thongs and peculiarities of modern taste : only the simplest
and most natural arrangements for the comfort of the inmates and their guests. Turkey carpets, steady round-tables,
and above all a sense of cheerful, hospitable kindness, which
seems to be traditional at Brantwood. For many years past
Mrs. Severn has kept her cousin's house, and welcomed his
guests with her own.

That evening — the first we spent at Brantwood — the
rooms were lighted by slow sunset cross-lights from the lake
without. Mrs. Severn sat in her place behind a silver urn,
while the master of the house, with his back to the window,
was dispensing such cheer, spiritual and temporal, as those
who have been his guests will best realize. Fine wheaten
bread and Scotch cakes in many a crisp circlet and crescent,
and trout from the lake, and strawberries such as only grow
on the Brantwood slopes. Were these cups of tea only, or
cups of fancy, feeling, inspiration? And as we crunched
and quaffed we listened to a certain strain not easily to be
described, changing from its graver first notes to the sweetest and most charming vibrations.

III

WHO can ever recall a good talk that is over? You can
remember the room in which it was held, the look of the
chairs, but the actual talk takes wings and flies away. A
dull talk has no wings, and is rememberd more easily ; so
are those tiresome conversations which consist of sentences
which we all repeat by rote, sentences which have bored us
a hundred times before, and which do not lose this property

by long use. But a real talk leaps into life; it is there almost before we are conscious of its existence. What system of notation can mark it down as it flows, modulating from its opening chords to those delightful exhilarating strains which are gone again almost before we have realized them.

Ruskin was explaining his views in his own words as we sat there. I should do him ill justice if I tried to transcribe his sermon. The text was that strawberries should be ripe and sweet, and we munched and marked it then and there; that there should be a standard of fitness applied to every detail of life; and this standard, with a certain gracious malice, wit, hospitality, and remorselessness, he began to apply to one thing and another, to one person and another, to dress, to food, to books. I remember his describing to my brother-in-law Leslie Stephen the shabby print and paper that people were content to live with, and contrasting with these the books he himself was then printing for the use of the shepherds round about. And among the rest he showed us Sir Philip Sidney's pharaphrase of the Psalms, which he has long since given to the world in the *Bibliotheca Pastorum*. Let us trust these fortunate shepherds are worthy of their print and margins.

If, as I have already said, we compare the talk of great men and women "who will cause this age to be remembered," one element is to be found in them all—a certain directness, simplicity, and vivid reality; a gift for reaching their hearers at once, giving light straight from themselves, and not in reflections from other minds; sunshine, in short, not moonshine. Perhaps something of this may be due to the habit of self-respect and self-reliance which success and strength of purpose naturally create. Many uncelebrated people have the grace of convincing simplicity, but I have never met a really great man without it. As one thinks of it, one recognizes that a great man is greater than we are

JOHN RUSKIN — [From portrait by Hubert Herkomer, A.R.A.]
From the etching published by Fine Art Society, London

because his aim (consciously or unconsciously) is juster, his strength stronger and less strained; his right is more right than ours, his certainty more certain; he shows us the best of that which concerns him, and the best of ourselves too in that which concerns *us* in his work or his teaching.

If we look at the Elgin marbles, for instance, we feel that the standard of human attainment is forever raised by those broken lines in eternal harmony, and we also indefinitely realize that while looking at them we ourselves are at our best in sculpture ; and so listening back to the echoes of a lifetime, we can most of us still hear some strains very clear, very real and distinct, out of all the confusion of past noise and chatter; and the writer (nor is she alone in this) must ever count the magic of the music of Brantwood oratory among such strains. Music, oratory, I know not what to call that wondrous gift which subjugates all who come within its reach.

"God uses us to help each other so, lending our minds out."

If ever a man lent out his mind to help others, Ruskin is the man. From country to country, from age to age, from element to element, he leads the way, while his audience, laughing, delighted, follows with scrambling thoughts and apprehensions and flying leaps, he meanwhile illustrating each delightful, fanciful, dictatorial sentence with pictures by the way—things, facts, objects interwoven, bookcases opening wide, sliding drawers unlocked with his own marvellous keys—and lo! we are perhaps down in the centre of the earth, far below Brantwood and its surrounding hills, among specimens, minerals, and precious stones, Ruskin still going ahead, and crying "sesame" and "sesame," and revealing each secret recess of his King's Treasury in turn, pointing to each tiny point of light and rainbow veined in marble, gold and opal, crystal and emerald. Then, perhaps, while we are wondering, and barely beginning to apprehend

E—2

his delightful illustrations, the lecturer changes from natural things to those of art, from veins of gold meandering in the marble and speaking of ages, to coins marking the history of man. I was specially struck by some lovely old Holbein pieces of Henry VIII. which he brought out. I can still see Ruskin's hand holding the broad gold mark in its palm. Who could help speculating at such a moment? Whence had it come, that golden token, since Holbein laid his chisel down? From what other hands had it reached this one? Had Shakespeare once had the spending of it, had Bacon clutched at it, or had Buckingham flung it to the wind, or had Milton owned it, perhaps, before Cromwell called the King's money back into his own treasury? Anyhow, this golden piece has escaped the Puritan's crucibles, and here it is still, to show us what a golden coin has been, and lying safe in the Brantwood treasury.

IV

IT is now several years since we were at Coniston, and I may have perhaps somewhat confused the various occasions when we went to Brantwood. One year the family was absent during our stay, but tokens of present kindness came day after day—basketfuls brought up by the gardener, roses and the afore-mentioned strawberries, and other ripe things that had colored in its sunshine.

Another year when we were staying at the farm Ruskin was at Brantwood, alone with a young relative, and he asked us to go up and see him. Again I remember one of those long monologues, varied, absorbing, combining pictures and metaphors into one delightful whole, while the talker, carried

LOOKING FROM BRANTWOOD TOWARDS THE HEAD OF CONISTON LAKE

along by his own interest in his subject, would be starting to his feet, bringing down one and another volume from the shelf, opening the page between his hands, and beginning to read the passage appropriate to his theme. It was some book of Indian warfare that he brought down from its place, and as he opened it he then and there began his sermon: spoke of the example which good Christian men and women might set in any part of the world; quoted Sir Herbert Edwards, whom he loved and admired, as an example of what a true man should be. He spoke of him with kindling eyes, warming as he went on to tell, as only a Ruskin could tell it, the heroic history of the first Sikh war. What happened in India yesterday he did not know; he said he sometimes spent months without once looking at the papers, and in deliberate ignorance of what was happening and not happening in their columns.

· There is a story told of Ruskin receiving a telegram not long ago from some member of the royal family, of which he could not construe the meaning until he called in the telegraph boy, who then informed him of an event with which the country had been ringing for weeks past, and to which the telegram related.

I further remember, among other things, after his little lecture upon "True Knights," a delightful description of what a True Lady should be. "A princess, a washer-woman," he said—"yes, a washer-woman! To see that all is fair and clean, to wash with water, to cleanse and purify wherever she goes, to set disordered things in orderly array—this was a woman's mission." Which sentence has often occurred to me since then at irritating moments of household administration. Ruskin has written something not unlike it in his lecture upon "Queen's Gardens;" but how different is the impression left, even by such printers' type as his, from that of the words and the voice flowing on in its measure!

The writer, speaking to one of Ruskin's most constant and faithful readers, once compared him to a Prospero, thinking of this strange power of his over the minds of those who are in his company, of the sweet harmonies he can raise at will, of the wanderings he can impose upon his subjects, and of his playful humors and fanciful experiments upon the audience, " be it to fly, to swim, to dive into the fire, to ride on the curl'd cloud." Mrs. Fanny Kemble, who was the lady in question (she sat with a volume of *Modern Painters* open before her), said: " No: I myself see no resemblance whatever between the two: Prospero dealt with magic and unreality ; the power of Ruskin lies in the extraordinary reality of his teaching. Think what a vision of beauty lies spread before that man." And this is certainly high and worthy praise, coming from one who herself belongs to the noble race of spiritual pastors and masters. Mrs. Kemble concluded by quoting Ruskin's account of a heap of gravel by the road-side, which she had just been reading, and which she said had struck her as one of the most remarkable descriptions ever written in the English language.

V

Ruskin has said somewhere that his three great masters have been Tintoret, Carlyle, and Turner. When John Ruskin, the son of John Ruskin, was born in 1819, Titian had been dead over two hundred years ; Carlyle, beginning life, was living in Edinburgh, where he was supporting himself by literature and by articles in Dr. Brewster's *Encyclopædia ;* Turner was a man of forty-four, already well advanced in life ; he had published his *Liber Studiorum*, painted many

noble pictures; he had built his
house in Queen Anne Street, and
was then starting for Italy. It was
a dull and unromantic time in the
history of England, a time reach-
ing beyond the fifty years' radius of our recent Jubilee.
Men, weary of war, were resting and counting its cost;
the poor were suffering, the rich were bankrupt; the old
King was dying, Princess Charlotte was dead; the Regent
was absorbed in his schemes and selfish ends; corn was
at starvation prices; mobs were breaking out in discon-
tent and riot; and yet no less than in more propitious
hours were the divine sparks falling from heaven—upon children at their play, upon infants in their cradles, who were
to grow up with hearts kindled by that sacred flame which,
refracted from generation to generation, keeps the world
alive.

> " See a disenchanted nation
> Spring like day from desolation ;
> To Truth its state is dedicate,
> And Freedom leads it forth."

So wrote Shelley, at that time looking his last at the Bay of Naples, and completing the first act of his *Prometheus*, while Browning and Tennyson were children at play in their fathers' gardens—Tennyson hidden far away among Lincolnshire wolds and levels, Browning plucking his own brand of Promethean fire somewhere on the heights that encircle the great city where Ruskin, still lying in his cradle, had not as yet found a miraculous voice to cry out with, and to protest that though love of Truth and Justice might be the same for both, Shelley's Freedom and John Ruskin's Freedom were as unlike as night and day.*

" I am, and my father was before me, a violent Tory of the old school—Walter Scott's school, that is to say, and Homer's," says Ruskin in the first lines of *Præterita*, going back to those early days when his lately married father and mother had settled down in Bloomsbury, and when he himself first comes upon the scene, "a child with yellow hair, dressed in a white frock like a girl, with a broad, light blue sash and blue shoes to match," standing at a window, and watching the events of the street.

As one reads *Præterita* it seems as if John Ruskin wrote his history not with ink, but painted it down with light and color; he brings the very atmosphere of his life and its phases before us with such an instantaneous mastery as few besides have ever reached—the life within, without the sweet eternal horizons (even though they be but Norwood

---

* " My own teaching has been and is that Liberty, whether in the body, soul, or political estate of men, is only another word for Death, and the final issue of Death— Putrefaction; the body, spirit, and political estate being healthy only by their bonds and laws."—1875, *Fors*, Letter 411.

hills and ridges), the living and delightful figures in the foreground.

Its author has chosen to christen the story *Præterita*, but was ever a book less belonging to the past and more entirely present to our mood than this one? Not Goethe's own autobiography, not even Carlyle's passionate reminiscences, come up to it in vividness. There are so few words, such limpid images are brought flashing before us, that in our secret consciousness we *remember* rather than we read." Are we not actually living in its pages, in the dawning light of that austere yet glorious childhood? Half a century rolls back, and we see the baby up above at the drawing-room windows, standing absorbed, watching the water-carts, and that wondrous turn-cock, "who turns and turns till a fountain springs up in the middle of the street," and as we still watch the child, gazing out with his blue, deep-set eyes, the brown brick walls somehow become transparent, as they did for Ebenezer Scrooge, and we are in the same mysterious fashion absorbed into the quiet home and silent life. We get to know the inmates with some immaterial friendship and intimacy. The father, "that entirely honest man" of rare gifts and refinement, going and coming to his wine-merchant's office in Billeter Street; the mother, combining the spirit of Martha and of Mary, unflinching, orderly, living for her husband and her son, not rejecting the better part, but forcing every member of her household to conform to *her* views of both worlds, and binding down their lives by some emphatic and restraining power. But how soon the child born to such liberty of thought, to such absolute obedience of will, learns to escape from his bonds, to create his own life and world! His very playthings (all others being denied to him) he makes for himself out of the elements, the air above, the waters beneath, the craters of the coal-heavers as they empty the sacks at the door. "My mother's general principles of the first treatment were to guard me with steady watchfulness from all avoidable pain or danger; and for the rest to let me amuse myself; but the law was I should find my own amusement. No toys of any kind were at first allowed, and the pity of my Croydon aunt for my monastic poverty in this respect was boundless. On one of my birthdays, thinking to overcome my mother's resolution by splendor of temptation, she bought the most radiant Punch and Judy she could find in all the Soho Bazar, as big as a real Punch and Judy, all dressed in scarlet and gold, and that would dance. . . . My mother was obliged to accept them, but afterwards quietly told me it was not right I should have them, and I never saw them again."

This Croydon aunt must have been a good and loving aunt to little John. "Whenever my father was ill," he says —" and hard work and sorrow had already set their mark on him — we all went down to Croydon to be petted by my homely aunt, and walk on Duppas Hill and on the heather of Addington." He dwells with affectionate remembrance upon the house and its gables and early fascinations for him. "My chosen domain being the shop, the back room, and the stones round the spring of crystal water at the back door (long since let down into the modern sewer), and my chief companion my aunt's dog Towser, whom she had taken pity on when he was a snappish, starved vagrant, and made a brave and affectionate dog of, which was the kind of thing she did for every living creature that came in her way all her life long."

Mrs. Ruskin, with all her passionate devotion to her son, seems to have had no idea whatever of making a little child happy. The baby's education was terribly consistent; he was steadily whipped when he was troublesome or when he tumbled down-stairs. "We seldom had company even on week-days, and I was never allowed to come down to dessert until much later in life, when I was able to crack other people's nuts for them, but never to have any myself, nor anything else of a dainty kind. Once at Hunter Street I recollect my mother giving me three raisins in the forenoon out of the store-cabinet." But not all the rules and rails and restrictions of Hunter Street and Brunswick Square could prevent the child from finding out for himself that brick walls do not a prison make, nor iron bars a cage. He stands in the light of the window, in his silent, thoughtful fashion, creating his own existence for himself, and just as the turn-cock turned and turned until a fountain sprang from the pavement, so even in baby life does Ruskin lay his master-hand upon the stones, and lo! the stream of life begins to flow. In later days he smites the rock, and bids the children drink living waters from the spring of life eternal, sometimes also to be mingled with those waters of strife "called Meribah." *

VI

IT was up on the summit of Herne Hill that John Ruskin the elder (when he felt that his affairs justified him in so doing) bought the semi-detached house standing among the almond blossoms, from whence Ruskin dates the preface to *Præterita*. "I write these few prefatory words on my father's birthday," says Ruskin, in the year 1886, "in what was once my nursery in his old house, to which he brought my mother and me sixty-two years since, I being then four years old."

We have good reason to be grateful to a writer who sets down for our happy reading such remembrance, such silence,

* See the first volume of *Modern Painters* and certain numbers of *Deucalion*, etc.

as this. Almost every child has some natural glamour and instinct of its own by which the glare of life is softened, and the first steep ways garlanded and eased and charmed. We call those men poets who retain this divine faculty all their lives, and who are able to continue looking at the world with the clear gaze of childhood, discerning the unchanging natural things and beauties in the midst of all the wanderings of disappointment and confusion. Such a poet is Ruskin, if ever a man was born one. Take the story of little John at play in his childish garden, where the mulberry-tree and the white heart cherry-tree are growing: "The ground was absolutely beneficent with magical splendor of abundant fruit, fresh green, soft amber, and rough bristled crimson, bending the spinous branches, clustered pearl and pendent ruby, joyfully discoverable under the large leaves that looked like vine." . . . "The differences of primal importance which I observed," he says, " between the nature of this garden and that of Eden, as I imagined it, were that in this one *all* the fruit was forbidden, and there were no companionable beasts." Then follows a touch of which many a parent will ruefully acknowledge the truth : "My mother, finding her chief personal pleasure in her flowers, was often planting or pruning beside me, at least if I chose to stay beside her. . . . Her presence was no restraint to me, and also no particular pleasure, for, from having always been left so much alone, I had generally my own little affairs to see to, and by the time I was seven years old I was already independent mentally both of my father and mother, and having nobody else to be dependent upon, began to lead a very small, poky, contented, conceited, Cock-Robinson-Crusoe sort of life."

How these words set one to the measure and the feeling of that isolated mystical little life in the central point of the universe, as he says it appeared to him, as it must generally appear to geometrical animals !

CONISTON—OLD HALL AND OLD MAN

When little John grew older he learned to read and to spell with what seems absolutely wonderful quickness. Every morning after breakfast he sat down with his mother to read the Bible. "My mother never gave me more to learn than she knew I could easily get learned, if I set myself honestly to work, by twelve o'clock. She never allowed anything to disturb me when my task was set; and in general, even when Latin grammar came to supplement the Psalms, I was my own master for at least half an hour before the half-past one dinner." The list of those portions of the Psalms and chapters of the Bible which little John Ruskin had to learn by heart is conscientiously given, and might seem to some of us an appalling list. But upon this he comments as follows: "Truly, though I have picked up the elements of a little further knowledge, and owe not a little to the teaching of many people, this maternal installation of my mind in that property of chapters I count very confidently the most precious, and on the whole the one essential, part of my education." "Peace, Obedience, Faith," were the three great boons of his early life, he says, and "the habit of fixed attention." The defects of it are told very forcibly in language which is pathetic in its directness. "I had nothing to love. My parents were, in a sort, visible powers of nature to me; no more loved than the sun and moon." And thus he sums it up. His life was too formal and too luxurious; "by protection innocent, instead of by practice virtuous."

Ruskin should have been a novelist. It is true, he says he never knew a child more incapable than himself of telling a tale, but when he chooses to describe a man * or a woman, there stands the figure before us; when he tells a

* Take these few lines descriptive of Severn: "Lightly sagacious, lovingly humorous, daintily sentimental, as if life were but for him the rippling chant of his favorite song, ' Gente ! è qui l'uccellatore.' "

story, we live it. His is rather the descriptive than the constructive faculty; his mastery is over detail and quality rather than over form. How delightfully he remembers! How one loves his journeys in Mr. Telford's post-chaise, where he sits propped upon his own little trunk between father and mother, looking out at the country through the glass windows. Mr. Ruskin the elder is travelling for orders, and he brings his family north, and finally to his sister's home in Perth, where we read of the Scottish aunt and the playfellow cousins, of the dark pools of Tay, of the path above them, "being seldom traversed by us children, except at harvest-time, when we used to go gleaning in the fields beyond." "I hesitate in recording as a constant truth for the world the impression left on me, when I went gleaning with Jessie, that Scottish sheaves are more golden than are found in other lands, and that no harvests elsewhere visible to human eyes are so like the corn of heaven * as those of Strath Tay and Strath Earn."

Was ever story more simple, more pathetic, than the story of little Peter and his mother! "My aunt, a pure dove-priestess, if ever there was one, of Highland Dodona, was of a far gentler temper, but still to me remained at a wistful distance. She had been much saddened by the loss of three of her children before her husband's death. Little Peter especially had been the corner-stone of her love's building; and it was thrown down swiftly. White-swelling came in the knee; he suffered much, and grew weaker gradually, dutiful always, and loving, and wholly patient. She wanted him one day to take half a glass of port-wine, and took him on her knee and put it to his lips. 'Not now, mamma; in a minute,' said he, and put his head on her shoulder, and gave one long, low sigh, and died."

* Psalms, lxxviii., 24.

Little Peter's mother followed him before many years, and the rest of her children having passed one by one through the dark river, Mary, the only survivor, comes to live in the Ruskin household, "a serene additional neutral tint" in the home.

The two children read the Bible together, write abstracts of the sermons in the chapel at Walworth, which they attend. On the Sundays when the family remain at home the father reads Blair's sermons aloud, or if a clerk or customer dines with them, "the conversation in mere necessary courtesy would take the direction of sherry" (Dickens himself might have envied this touch), while the two children sit silent in their corner with the *Pilgrim's Progress* and Quarles's *Emblems* and Fox's *Book of Martyrs* to pass the time.

On week-days John, who is now ten years old, is learning Greek with Dr. Andrews, copying Cruikshank's illustrations, and writing English doggerel.

When Ruskin was turned twelve his mother had taken him six times through the Bible; he had had various classical masters, drawing masters, and other teachers; he had begun to study mineralogy, was allowed to taste wine, to go to a theatre, and on festive days to dine with his father and mother, and to listen to his father's reading of the *Noctes Ambrosianæ* and of Byron. On Ruskin's thirteenth birthday his father's partner, Mr. Henry Telford, gives him Rogers's *Italy*, with its illustrations, and, so he says, determined the main tenor of his life. "The drawing-master had vaguely stated that the world had been greatly dazzled and led away by some splendid ideas thrown out by Turner, but until then Turner had not existed for the quiet family on Herne Hill."

Besides all these rising interests there are also the descriptions of the people (not very numerous) who begin to cross the stage, we get glimpses of the neighbors, and we seem to know them as we know the people out of *Vanity Fair*, or out of Miss Austen's novels: Mr. Telford, the owner of the travelling carriage and the giver of illustrated books; the two clerks at their work—Henry Ritchie, who loves Margate—(If you want to be happy, get a wife and come to Margate, he writes)—and Henry Watson and his musical sisters. Then there is Miss Andrews, who sang "Tambourgi, Tambourgi;" old Mrs. Munroe, with Petite, her white poodle; and her daughter Mrs. Richard Gray, "entirely simple, meek, loving, and serious, saved from being stupid by a vivid nature full of enthusiasm, like her husband's." It is English middle-class life for the most part, described with something of George Eliot's racy reality.

VII

In the early chapters of *Præterita* there is the story of Ruskin's first acquaintance with the enchanting Domecq family, which played so important a part in his young life— the four girls who, arriving unexpectedly, reduced him "to a heap of white ashes," which *mercredi des cendres*, we read, lasted four years. We are not exactly told which of the sisters—whether Adele, the graceful blonde of fifteen, Cecile, the dark-eyed, finely browed girl of thirteen, or Elise or little Caroline of eleven, was the chief favorite. They had all been born abroad; they spoke Spanish and French with perfect grace, English with broken precision; he describes "a Southern Cross of unconceived stars floating on a sudden into my obscure firmament of a London suburb."

The writer can picture to herself something of the charm

ENTRANCE TO BRANTWOOD

of these most charming sisters, for once by chance, travelling on Lake Leman, she found herself watching a lady who sat at the steamer's end, a beautiful young woman, all dressed in pale gray, with a long veil floating on the wind, who sat motionless and absorbed, looking towards the distant hills, not unlike the vision of some guiding, wistful Ariel at the prow, while the steamer sped its way between the banks. The story of the French sisters has gained an added interest from the remembrance of those dark, lovely eyes, that charming countenance, for afterwards, when I knew her better, the lady told me that her mother had been a Domecq, and had once lived with her sisters in Mr. Ruskin's home. Circumstances had divided them in after-days, but all the children of the family in turn had been brought up to know Mr. Ruskin by name, and to love and appreciate his books. The lady sent him many messages by me, which I delivered in after-days, when, alas! it was from Mr. Ruskin himself I learned that the beautiful traveller—Isabelle, he called her—had passed away before her time to those distant hills where all our journeys end.

Ruskin's jubilee should be counted from the year 1833, when he tells us he went with his father to a shop to enter their names as subscribers to Prout's *Sketches in Flanders and Italy*, and they were shown the specimen print of the turreted window over the Moselle at Coblentz. "We got the book home to Herne Hill before the time of our usual annual tour, and as my mother watched my father's pleasure and mine in looking at the wonderful places, she said, why should not we go and see some of them in reality? My father hesitated a little, and then, with glittering eyes, said, why not?" How plainly one can see the picture! The little family assembled in its quiet after-dinner conclave, the boy turning over the pages of his book, the father opening the big map, the practical mother transforming dreams into reality. Quiet and monotonous lives lend themselves more readily than more brilliant existences to possibilities, to immense events, and this was an event for all the world as well as for the Ruskin family.

Was there ever, will there ever be such a journey again, such a combination of comfort, of dawning genius, of actual dignity and leisure, of eyes to see, of wheels to roll smoothly along the broad roads? The child no longer sits perched on his improvised little bracket-seat, but is one of a dignified family with a maid and courier travelling as quickly as four horses and postilions in huge boots can carry them towards the wonder-land beyond the horizon, that country of vines, of distant Alpine ranges, of cloud and sky and mountain pass, of fair city and glorious art.

He says: "We found our pleasant rooms always ready, our good horses always waiting; everybody took their hats off when we arrived and when we departed; Salvador presented his accounts weekly, and they were settled without a word of demur. To all these conditions of luxury and felicity can the modern steam-puffed tourist conceive the added and culminating one that we were never in a hurry?"

The story of Ruskin's first sight of the Alps is one that no one who has ever seen a snowy range will pass over or forget.

"We dined at four as usual, and the evening being entirely fine, went out to walk, all of us—my father and mother and Mary and I.

"We must have still spent some time in town-seeing, for it was drawing towards sunset when we got up to some garden promenade, west of the town, I believe, and high above the Rhone, so as to command the open country across it to the south and west, when suddenly—behold—beyond. There was no thought in any of us for a moment of their being clouds. They were clear as crystal, sharp on the pure horizon sky, and already tinged with rose by the sinking sun. Infinitely beyond all that we had ever thought or dreamed, the seen walls of Eden could not have been more beautiful to us; not more awful round heaven the walls of sacred Death. . . . Thus in perfect health of life and fire of heart, not wanting to have anything more than I had, knowing of sorrow only just so much as to make life serious to me, not enough to slacken in the least its sinews, and with so much of science mixed with feeling as to make the sight of the Alps not only the revelation of the beauty of the earth, but the opening of the first page of its volume, I went down that evening from the garden terrace of Schaffhausen with my destiny fixed in all of it that was to be most sacred and useful. To that terrace and to the shore of the Lake of Geneva my heart and faith return to this day in every impulse that is yet nobly alive in them, and every thought that has in it help or peace."

It would be too long to transcribe at length, as one would like to do, the pages of *Præterita* which take us from one lovely height to another, from summer to summer, from Schaffhausen to Milan, to the " encompassing Alps, the perfectness and purity of the sweet, stately, stainless marble against the sky."

We all build tabernacles here and there in life. It was on the Col de la Faucille that John Ruskin erected his in 1835.

"The Col de la Faucille on that day opened to me in distinct vision the Holy Land of my future work and true home in this world," he says. " Far as the eye could reach —that land and its moving or pausing waters; Arve, and his gates of Cluse, and his glacier fountains; Rhone, and the infinitude of his sapphire lake, his peace beneath the narcissus meads of Vevay, his cruelty beneath the promontories of Sierre. And all that rose against and melted into the sky, of mountain and mountain snow; and all that living plain, burning with human gladness, studded with white houses, a Milky Way of star dwellings cast across its sunlit blue." *

And so we are able to follow the child year by year; we see little John grow from out his blue shoes and ribbons, *via* frilled collars and boyish buttons, to rustling dignities of silken robe and tasselled cap, and promoted from his niche behind the drawing-room chimney-piece to the run of all the cloisters of Oxford. His father meanwhile returns contentedly to his desk opposite the brick wall, where he sits

* The following fac-simile note in allusion to the above was written long after:

quietly amassing the fortune he spends so generously and in so liberal a spirit.

The history of the Turners is also to be noted : of the collection gradually increasing ; of the father's pleasure, of the son's delight, in the pictures of Richmond Bridge and Gosport ; in the drawing of Winchelsea, " the chief recreation of my fatigued hours." Sir John Simon tells a story of a visit Ruskin once paid to a sale of pictures, and of his return home dispirited, saying there was but one picture he had wanted in the whole collection, and that one was already sold. And there it was before him. It was his father who had bought it, thinking it was one he would be sure to delight in. Ruskin the elder must have had a most unerring and remarkable critical faculty, and it was undoubtedly from him that John Ruskin inherited his own genius for art. There is the record of the paternal gift of £200 a year in the funds upon the son's coming of age, out of which another Turner is bought for £70. " It was not a piece of painted paper, but a Welsh castle and village and Snowdon in blue cloud that I bought for my seventy pounds."

VIII

RUSKIN was entered as Gentleman-Commoner at Christchurch, Oxford, and came up in January, 1837. " I was entered as Gentleman-Commoner without further debate, and remember still as if it were yesterday the pride of walking out of the Angel Hotel and past University College, holding my father's arm, in my velvet cap and silk gown."

The father and mother had set their hearts on his going

into the Church. He would have made a bishop, said his
father long years after, with tears in his eyes; and we may
read now, indeed, of the first sermon Ruskin ever preached,
a baby one, in which he describes himself as standing up
with a red cushion before him, and thumping and preach-
ing " People be good." *

Ruskin remained at Oxford until 1840. The story of
his stay there, of his work, of his friends, is all delightful
reading; not the least touching part of it all is the account
of his mother (with his father's entire acquiescence) leaving
her home, her daily habits, and establishing herself in lodgings in the Oxford High Street, so as to be at hand in case
of need. Ruskin's own filial devotion is also to be admired.
He tells us that his wishes and his happiness were the chief
preoccupations of their lives, and he accepts the loving tie
generously, as all sons do not. Speaking of his degree,
Ruskin says : " When I was sure I had got through, I went
out for a walk in the fields north of New College (since
turned into the Parks), happy in the sense of recovered
freedom, but extremely doubtful to what use I should put
it. There I was at two-and-twenty, with such and such
powers, all second-rate except the analytical ones, which
were as much in embryo as the rest, and which I had no
means of measuring; such and such likings hitherto in-
dulged rather against conscience, and a dim sense of duty
to myself, my parents, and a daily more vague shadow of
Eternal Law. What should I be or do?" This question
was to be answered very shortly by publication of the first
volume of *Modern Painters*. Before coming away from Oxford I must not omit to quote a curious passage concerning
Dean Liddell, "one of the rarest types of nobly presenced
Englishmen, the only man in Oxford in his day who cared

* Nor, indeed, has he happily ceased to preach this sermon, the text of which brings
back to one's mind the touching words of dying Scott.

about art, and whose 'keen' saying concerning Turner, 'that he had got hold of a false ideal,'" is here noted (curiously enough) by Ruskin as one which would have been eminently helpful to him at the time, had it been then impressed upon him. After that we come to the history of that illness after overwork which sent Ruskin and his parents abroad again for an indefinite period, travelling away by Rouen and Tours. by the Rhone to Avignon, thence by the Riviera to Florence and the South, in search of health. There is also this epitaph upon Oxford: "Oxford taught me as much Greek as she could, and though I think she might have also told me that fritillaries grew in Iffley meadow, it was better that she left me to find them for myself. I must get on," he continues, "to the days of opening sight and effective labor, and to the scenes of nobler education, which all men who keep their hearts open receive in the end of days."

It is always interesting to ascertain when a great man begins his life's work; but, after all, it is scarcely the printing of the book or the framing of the picture which puts a date to the hour in which the mind ripens or carries out its conception; and the casual mention in *Præterita* of the publication of *Modern Painters* shows how much of thought and feeling had already gone towards the book, of which the actual publishing seemed the least memorable part to the author. Speaking of the first volume of *Modern Painters*, he only says: "It took the best part of the winter's leisure," and dismisses the subject with, "The said first volume must have been out by my father's birthday; its success was assured by the end of the year."

The book made its mark then and there. Those qualities which Ruskin prefers to call his analytical qualities seem to others to be a happy combination of intuition, of industry, and vivid imagination. Though the graduate's principles and teachings were variously esteemed, every one acknowledged their importance, and it seems but justice to Mr. Ruskin to suggest that he was not altogether accountable for the seriousness with which his admirers have sometimes accepted his eloquent paradoxes and humors. It is hardly fair, perhaps, to look back at the by-gone criticisms of this startling and eloquent publication. Reviewers writing long after, with experience and knowledge of the road, can drive their team steadily, cracking their long whips with a sense of dignity and final authority which is admirable for retrospective commonplace; but how are they to rein in a Pegasus who has inadvertently found himself harnessed to the old coach, and who puts out his wings and flies straight up into the air? Pegasus in his flight does not hesitate to kick out right and left, overturning as he goes the various "Van Somethings and Bac Somethings," with other shrines that we would more gladly sacrifice. *Blackwood* of those days took up the battle in an overbearing and angry spirit. The reviewer comes to the defence of the giants and windmills this new Don Quixote is attacking right and left—Claude, Salvator, Cuyp, Berghem, Ruysdael, etc. "You cannot judge with judgment if you have not the sun in your spirit and passion in your heart," cries the young champion, dealing his thrusts. But this is not language to be applied to such authorities as those of *Blackwood* then, or perhaps of the *Edinburgh* nowadays; and the critics in return strike at the graduate with the sun in their eyes, and with passion in their words if not in their hearts.

A second article which appeared in *Blackwood* some years later was far more within the limits of fair and measured criticism, allowing the book to be the work of a man of power, thinking independently, feeling strongly, and with "a mortal aversion to be in a crowd." Meanwhile *Fraser*, in its article on the second edition, declares that "the Oxford graduate has sought a reputation even in the cannon's mouth, has scaled the wall of the Castle of Prejudice, and from its embattled parapet waves us to follow." The graduate's volume "prompts us to leave the conventional for the true, and quitting the cant of gallery connoisseurship, to find tongues in trees, books in the running brooks, sermons in stones, and good in everything." From the *Ethics of the Dust* to the *Stones of Venice*, from the *Springs of Wandel* to *Deucalion*, there is nothing which has once attracted him which he does not study with love and intuition, nothing he does not use with admiration. This applies most especially to his love for Nature. For the more human part in art his feeling is different altogether, and there his instinct for destruction is often as fierce as his gift for construction is exquisite when he treats of Nature and her silent belongings.

IX

THE writer of this little essay certainly cannot pretend either to the knowledge or to the infallibility of an art critic, and she has therefore ventured to take Ruskin from her own point of view only, as a "Light-bearer," as a writer of the English language, as a poet in his own measure. How is it possible to a man writing, as he says, "with passion," with all the vibrating chords of a thousand interests and revelations, to be the temperate and dispassionate awarder of that bare justice which is all an orthodox critic should bestow? Many things, indeed, leave him altogether silent and apparently irresponsive; he does not always contradict the verdict of generations, but he accepts it without enthusiasm. The instinctive form which beauty takes for him is that of Nature and her direct influence upon himself. His attitude towards

Greek art is curiously characteristic of this; so were his first impressions of Rome.

Very long afterwards Ruskin said of his mother's house-keeping arrangements: "I don't think the reader has yet been informed that I inherited to the full my mother's love of tidiness and cleanliness, and that in Switzerland, next to her eternal snows, what I most admired was her white sleeves."

Was it Ruskin's love of order, then, which caused him to suffer so much in Rome, where he waywardly painted the rags fluttering in a by-street, and would not give a thought to the ancient churches and statues and pictures and ruins? Was it his love of tidiness or his sincerity which made him at first write almost cruelly of Italy, of Florence, and of the Uffizi, of Siena and its cathedral, "costly confectionery, faithless vanity?" The first sight of St. Peter's, he tells us, was to him little more than a gray milestone, announcing twenty miles yet of stony road. He ascertained that the Stanze could not give him any pleasure. "What the Forum or Capitol had been he did not in the least care. Raphael's 'Transfiguration' and Domenichino's 'St. Jerome' he pronounced, without the smallest hesitation — Domenichino's a bad picture, and Raphael's an ugly one" (which verdict I can remember my own father indorsing, as far as the Raphael was concerned). I ought also in fairness to add that, later on, many of Ruskin's unqualified early criticisms are entirely modified and swept away.

For the second volume of *Modern Painters*, "not meant to be in the least like what it is," Ruskin wanted "more Chamouni;" and further on, feeling that he must know more of Italy, see Pau and Florence again, before writing another word, he tells his indulgent parents of his wish. Turner, of all people, strongly opposed the journey, the Continent being then in an angry and disturbed condition; but papa and mamma seem to have agreed. And so the new life began for him as we read in the chapters headed Campo Santo and Macugnaga. "Serious, enthusiastic, worship and wonder and work; up at six, drawing, studying, thinking; breaking bread and drinking wine at intervals: homeward the moment the sun went down." "The days that began in the cloister of the Campo Santo at Pisa ended by my getting upon the roof of Santa Maria della Spina, and sitting in the sunlight that tranfused the warm marble of its pinnacles till the unabated brightness went down beyond the arches of the Ponte a Mare, the few footsteps and voices of the twilight silent in the streets, and the city and her mountains stood mute as a dream beyond the soft eddying of Arno." We may judge by these illustrations to his life what sort of material it was that Ruskin himself put into his noble books.

It was between the publication of the first and second volumes of *Modern Painters* that Ruskin came under Carlyle's influence. Long years afterwards Carlyle himself, writing to Emerson, says: "There is nothing going on among us as notable to me as those fierce lightning-bolts Ruskin is copiously and desperately pouring into the black world of Anarchy all around him. No other man in England that I meet has in him the divine rage against iniquity, falsity, and baseness that Ruskin has, and that every man ought to have. Unhappily he is not a strong man—one might say a weak man rather—and has not the least prudence of management, though if he can hold out for another fifteen years or so, he may produce, even in this way, a great effect or so. God grant it, say I."

I heard a pretty account once from Mr. Alfred Lyttelton of a visit paid by Ruskin to Carlyle in the familiar room in Cheyne Walk, with the old picture of Cromwell on the wall, and Mrs. Carlyle's little tables and pretty knickknacks still in their quiet order. Mr. Ruskin had been ill not long before, and as he talked on of something he cared about, Mr. Lyttelton said his eyes lighted up, and he seemed agitated and moved. Carlyle stopped him short, saying the subject was too interesting. "You must take care," he said, with that infinite kindness which Carlyle could show; "you will be making yourself ill once more." And Ruskin, quite simply, like a child, stopped short. "You are right," he said, calling Carlyle "master," and then went on to talk of something else, as dull, no doubt, as anything could be that Ruskin and Carlyle could talk about together.

In the first volume of *Præterita* there is one particular passage about Carlyle to which many of us will demur.

Ruskin himself this time is now quoting from the Emerson correspondence, and he says: "I find at page 18 this to me entirely disputable, and to my thought, so far as undisputed, much blamable and pitiable exclamation of my master's: 'Not till we can think that here and there one is thinking of us, one is loving us, does this waste earth become a peopled garden.' My training, as the reader has perhaps enough perceived, produced in me the precisely opposite sentiment. My times of happiness had always been when nobody was thinking of me. . . . The garden at home was no waste place to me because I did not suppose myself an object of interest either to the ants or the butterflies, and the only qualification of the delight of my evening walk at Champagnole was the sense that my father and mother *were* thinking of me, and would be frightened if I was ten minutes late for tea. . . .

"I don't mean in the least that I could have done without them. They were to me much more than Carlyle's wife to him. . . . But that the rest of the world was waste to him unless he had admirers in it is a sorry state of sentiment enough, and I am somewhat tempted for once to admire the exactly opposite temper of my own solitude. My entire delight was in observing without being observed ; if I could have been invisible, all the better. I was absolutely interested in men and in their ways as I was interested in marmots and chamois and in trouts. . . . The living habitation of the world, the grazing and nesting in it, the spiritual power of the air, the rocks, the waters—to be in the midst of it, and rejoice, and wonder at ; . . . this was the essential love of nature in me, this the root of all that I have usefully become."

As I have already said, this peculiar sense of solemn responsibility to nature and to mankind, and irresponsibility to individuals, is most specially to be noted in Ruskin ; more specially in the young Ruskin, who writes as people of strong imaginations write when the impulse is on them, realizing at the moment but one aspect of a feeling. But though he writes in this detached and lofty fashion, every page of his memoir vibrates with the warm light of a united home, where exist mutual love, confidence, sympathy, without which half the charm of the whole picture would be gone.

X

At Macugnaga, Ruskin, maturing his second volume, seems to have lived in good company, with a couple of Shakespeare's plays and his own thoughts, but not to have enjoyed his solitude so much as might have been expected from his theories. Mr. Boxall and Mr. Hardinge presently joined him for a time, and then came another serious illness, after which the second volume of *Modern Painters* was published, in 1846.

This second volume concerns the schools of Italy and its histories of art, and raised as much indignation as the first had done, though less irritation. Critics thanked Heaven openly that they were publicans and still able to admire, not Pharisees rejecting right and left. Then followed another beautiful sermon and more parables. "The book I called *The Seven Lamps* was to show that certain right states of temper and moral feeling were the magic powers by which all good architecture, without exception, had been produced." *The Stones of Venice* appeared between the years 1851 and 1853, and had from beginning to end no other aim than to show that the Gothic architecture of Venice had arisen out of, and indicated in all its features, a state of pure national faith and of domestic virtue, and that its Renaissance architecture had arisen out of, and indicated in all its features, a state of concealed national infidelity and of domestic corruption.

Again and again, as we read our Ruskin, the truth of his father's saying occurs to one, "He should have been a bishop!" Everything has a moral to him and a meaning. "In these books of mine, their distinctive character as essays on art is their bringing everything to a root in human passion or in human hope," he says in *Modern Painters* (vol. v.). The law of perfectness is one of his favorite texts, one that he would have us all pursue. He culls and he chooses at will, dwelling upon each detail which illustrates his own vast and lovely conception of things as they should be—as they *might* be for us if we were all Ruskins; and the chief danger for his disciples is that of seeing details too vividly, and missing the whole. There is also all the extraordinary influence of his personality in his teaching. Oracles such as Mill and Spencer veil their faces when they utter. Poets and orators like Ruskin uncover their heads as they address their congregations.

Ruskin has not only words at his command, but delicate hands. Look at the sketches and drawings in the latter volumes of *Modern Painters*. How eloquent and graceful they are, whether it is indicated motion or shadow, whether clouds or spiral leaf and upspringing branch!

When Ruskin records his past, it is as often as not by the sketches he has taken along the way that he marks his progress. And how true the saying is that nothing else—no descriptions—ever bring back a former state of mind and being as an old sketch will do! Sometimes one's old self actually seems to come up and take it out of one's hand. Only last night, apropos of these sketches of Ruskin's, and of a new portfolio of them lately published, I heard no less an authority than the Slade Professor at Cambridge saying that, with all the credit Professor Ruskin has justly won as a master of English diction, he has scarcely gained as much as he deserved for the exquisite character of his actual drawing.

As one looks down the list of Ruskin's writings* one can

---

* It may be convenient to give the following list of Mr. Ruskin's works, taken from *Men of the Time*, and from the fly-leaves of Mr. George Allen:

Poems. Friendship's Offering. 1835 to 1843.
Modern Painters. Vol. I., 1843.
Modern Painters. Vol. II., 1846.
Art. *Quarterly Review*, June, 1847, Lord Lindsay's Christian Art March, 1848, Eastlake on the History of Painting.
Seven Lamps of Architecture.
King of the Golden River. 1849. Illustrated by R. Doyle.
Stones of Venice. Vol. III., '51-'53. 1851.
Lectures on Architecture and Painting. 1853.
Giotto and his Works in Padua, 1854, for the Arundel Society.
Notes on the Royal Academy. Five parts. 1855 to 1859.
Modern Painters. Vol. III., 1856.
Modern Painters. Vol. IV., 1856.
Notes on the Turner Collection. 1857.
Political Economy of Art. 1857. Two Lectures. 1859-1860.
The Two Paths. (Lectures on Art.)
Modern Painters. Vol. V., 1860.
Sir Joshua Holbein. *Cornhill Magazine*. 1860.

Unto this Last. *Cornhill Magazine*. 1860-1862.
Munera Pulveris. *Frazer's Magazine*. 1862-1863.
Notes on the Alps.
Cestus of Aglaia. 1865.
Sesame and Lilies. 1865.
Ethics of the Dust. 1865.
Crown of Wild Olive. 1866.
Time and Tide by Wear and Tyne.
Queen of the Air. 1869.
Lectures on Art. 1871 to 1878.
Fors Clavigera.
Aratra Pentelice. 1872.
The Relation between Michael Angelo and Tintoret. 1872.
The Eagle's Nest. 1872.
Ariadne Florentina. 1873-1876.
Love's Meinie. 1873.
Val d' Arno. 1874.
Proserpina. 1875-1876.
Deucalion. 1875-1878.
Mornings in Florence. 1875-1877.
Bibliotheca Pastorum. 1877.
Præterita. (Still publishing.) 1888.

roughly read the story of his life. In the early numbers of the *Cornhill Magazine* his papers on political economy appeared, and it must have been about that time that he entered into his partnership with Miss Octavia Hill, resulting in one of the most important and interesting movements of the day.

There is a short article by Miss Hill in a by-gone *Fortnightly Review*, describing the beginning of what has led to so much. The article is called "Cottage Property in London." The said cottages, begrimed, and overcrowded by the dreary London peasantry, were whitewashed and drained with the help of Mr. Ruskin's £700, and relet again by Miss Hill to the poor people themselves, of whom she always writes with admirable discernment and sympathy. As she tells of her tenants, of their fortitude, their power of hope, their simple, entire confidence, their extraordinary patience, Miss Hill speaks with the knowledge that people bring whose genius is in the work into which they throw their hearts, and Mr. Ruskin was the first to recognize her gift.

"I had not great ideas of what must be done," she says. "My strongest endeavors were to be used to rouse habits of industry and effort. The plan was one which depended on just governing more than on helping. The first point was to secure such power as would enable me to insist on some essential sanitary arrangements. I laid the scheme before Mr. Ruskin, who entered into it most warmly. He at once came forward with all the money necessary, and took the whole risk of the undertaking upon himself. He showed me, however, that it would be far more useful if it could be made to pay—that a workingman ought to be able to pay for his own house." . . .

I found a letter among my father's papers the other day which must have been written by Mr. Ruskin about this time, and as it bears upon one of his many theories, and is interesting and characteristic, I will insert it here. It concerned an old friend of my father's, Monsieur Louis Marvy, who spent one winter in Young Street. He was an engraver by profession; he had, as I believe, been mixed up in some of the revolutionary episodes of 1848. He was a very charming and gentle person, in delicate health. He used to work hour after hour at his plates. He lived quietly in our house, chiefly absorbed by his work. He died quite young, not long after his return to France. Mr. Ruskin's letter refers in a measure to this by-gone episode, and I have his permission to transcribe it :

"DENMARK HILL, 21st December, 1860.

"DEAR MR. THACKERAY,—I think (or should think if I did not know) that you are quite right in this general law about lecturing, though, until I knew it, I did not feel able to refuse the letter of request asked of me.

"The mode in which you direct your charity puts me in mind of a matter that has lain long on my mind, though I never have had the time or face to talk to you of it.

"In somebody's drawing-room ages ago you were speaking accidentally of M. de Marvy. I expressed my great obligation to him, on which you said that I could now prove my gratitude, if I chose, to his widow, which choice I then not accepting, have ever since remembered the circumstance as one peculiarly likely to add, so far as it went, to the general impression on your mind of the hollowness of people's sayings and hardness of their hearts.

"The fact is, I give what I give almost in an opposite way to yours. I think there are many people who will relieve hopeless distress for one who will help at a hopeful pinch, and when I have choice I nearly always give where I think the money will be fruitful rather than merely helpful. I would lecture for a school when I would *not* for a distressed author, and would have helped De Marvy to perfect his invention, but not—unless I had no other object—his widow after he was gone. In a word, I like to prop the falling more than to feed the fallen. This, if you ever find out anything of my private life, you will know to be true ;

but I shall never feel comfortable, nevertheless, about that Marvy business unless you send to me for ten pounds for the next author, or artist, or widow of either, whom you want to help.

"And with this weight at last off my mind, I pray you to believe me always faithfully, respectfully yours,   J. Ruskin.

"All best wishes of the season to you and your daughters."

And my father's daughter may be perhaps forgiven for adding that there are few among us who will not sympathize as much with Mr. Ruskin when he breaks his theories as when he keeps to them. I don't know if it is fair to quote the story I heard at Coniston, long after, of the man who had grossly lied and cheated at Brantwood for years, and whose wages Mr. Ruskin went on paying, because he could not give him a character, and could not let him and his children starve.

XI

It may be here as well to say a few words of Mr. Ruskin's public work. In the statement of the purposes of St. George's Guild published by him he explains the two chief objects of the society :—Firstly, agricultural work, reclaiming waste lands, and the encouragement of manual labor without the help of steam ("a cruel and furious waste of fuel to do what every stream and breeze are ready to do"); Secondly, the building of museums and schools of art and study. "I continually see subscriptions of ten, fifteen, or twenty thousand pounds for new churches. Now a good clergyman never wants a church. He can say all his parishioners essentially need to hear in any of his parishioners' best parlors or upper chambers, or, if these are not large enough, in the market-place or harvest-field. What does he want with altars—was the Lord's Supper eaten on one?—what with pews—useless rents for the pride of them; what with font and pulpit that the next way-side brook or mossy bank cannot give him?". . . In order to form wholesome habits they (the young) must be placed under wholesome conditions. For the pursuit of any intellectual inquiry to advantage not only leisure must be granted them but quiet. . . . The words "school," "college," "university," rightly understood, imply the leisure necessary for learning, the companionship necessary for sympathy, and wilfulness restrained by the daily vigilance and firmness of tutors and masters.

The writer has not seen the museum at Sheffield, but happening to admire the work of a young water-color painter only a day ago, and to ask where he had studied, she was told that he had studied with nature for a teacher; but that besides working in this great academy he had also greatly profited by Mr. Ruskin's museum at Sheffield, where the most interesting and valuable art treasures are to be found in a couple of rooms opening on each side of the door of a road-side cottage. At one time Mr. Ruskin intended to build an art museum for Sheffield, and commissioned Mr. William Marshall to prepare the plans. I do not know why this scheme was never carried beyond the designs. Oxford first elected him to the Slade Professorship. Cambridge also made signals of respect and admiration, and he was elected Rede Lecturer in 1867. But it is difficult to imagine Ruskin at Cambridge; Oxford seems to belong far more to his genius, to his emotional gifts, his playful mediæval and romantic views of life. I have heard of him entertaining his guests as hospitably in his rooms at Corpus as at Brantwood by the waters of the lake. A friend described to us the well-served breakfast, ample beyond all appetite of host or guest, and Ruskin, fearing to disappoint the cook, sending friendly and appreciative messages. "A very nice relish for breakfast, sir," says the scout, offering some particular dish. "A very nice relish at any time," says Ruskin, kindly, refusing, "and tell the cook I said so."

The following note of welcome shows what trouble Brantwood takes for its friends:

"KING'S ARMS, LANCASTER, *Saturday.*

"DEAR MR. ——,—I have left orders to make you comfortable ; it is just possible, after these two days of darkness, you may even have a gleam of sun on Monday morning.

"Eleven train to Carnforth Junction, where change carriages for Ulverstone, where getting out, you will, I doubt not, see a dark post-chaise, into which getting, an hour and a half's pleasant drive brings you to Brantwood, where I hope you may be not uncomfortable whatever the weather.

"Yours faithfully, J. RUSKIN."

Not the least among Ruskin's gifts to his fellow-men are the beautiful copies of beautiful pictures which he has had executed for the students at Sheffield and elsewhere : the best copies that the best talent art and knowledge could produce, bestowed with like liberality and sympathy upon those who have no means of reaching the originals. The following letters relating to this work will be found interesting. One is struck by the care for the work and the interest in the worker, to whose great kindness I owe this record :

"OXFORD, *20th May,* 1873.

"MY DEAR ——,—I have your interesting letter, with the (to me very charming) little sketch of 'The Peace.' By the Virtues *on the left* I meant what perhaps my memory fails in placing there — on the left-hand wall, standing with your back to the window. 'The Peace' is opposite window, isn't it ? I can only say, do any face that strikes you.

In this composition I care more for completeness of record than for accurate copying. There is nothing in it that I esteem exquisite as painting ; but all is invaluable as design and emotion. Do it as thoroughly as you can pleasantly to yourself. For me, the Justice and Concord are the importantest. As you have got to work comfortably on it, don't hurry. Do it satisfactorily ; and then to Assisi, where quite possibly I may join you, though not for a month or six weeks.

"Keep me well in knowledge of your health and movements (writing now to Coniston), and believe me

"Very faithfully yours, J. RUSKIN.

. . . "I shall soon be writing to the good monks at Assisi; give them my love always.

"Do not spare fees to custodes, and put them down separately to me.

"People talk so absurdly about bribing. An Italian cannot know at first anything about an Englishman but that he is either stingy or generous. The money gift really opens his heart, if he has one. You can do it in that case without money, indeed, eventually, but it is amazing how many people can have good (as well as bad) brought out of them by gifts, and no otherwise."

"LONDON, 15th June, 1873.

"MY DEAR ——,—I am very glad to have your letters, and to see that you are on the whole well, and happy in your work. One's friends never do write to one when one's at Siena ; somehow it is impossible to suppose a letter ever gets there.

"You may stay at your work there as long as you find necessary for easy completion. It will be long before I get to Assisi.

"I don't care about anything in the Villa Spanocchi. All my pleasant thoughts of it — or any other place nearly — are gone. Do ' The Peace' as thoroughly as possible, now you are at it.

"I have intense sympathy with you about Sunday, but fancy my conscience was unusually morbid. I am never comfortable on the day. Of course the general shop-shutting and dismalness in England adds to the effect of it.

"Your day is admirably laid out, except that in your walk after four you go to look at pictures. You ought to rest in changed thoughts as much as possible, to get out on the green banks and brows, and think of nothing but what the leaves and winds say.

"I have nothing to tell you of myself that is pleasant ; not much that

H

is specially otherwise. The weather has been frightful in London. It was better at Coniston, but it appalls me ; it is a plague of darkness such as I never believed nature could inflict or suffer.

"Always affectionately yours, J. RUSKIN."

"HERNE HILL, 23d *April*, 1882.

. . . "That is a good passage of Leonardo's, but if you had read my Oxford lectures you would find their whole initiatory line and shade practice is (with distinct announcement of his authority) based on his book. I had read every word of it with care before I finished *Mod. P.*"

XII

SIR CHARLES NEWTON writes on one occasion : "I spent last night with Ruskin, and very delightful it was. He is now taking that larger view of art which I always expected he would, and begins to regard Greek art from the point of view in which it ought to be looked at, and was regarded by the Greeks themselves." This letter was shown me by the kindest of friends, whose own noble inspiration is a blessing and a light to the age. Watts has often described his discussions with Ruskin during their long and intimate companionship. That Ruskin is remorseless all his friends must allow, but he is remorseless to himself as soon as a conviction is borne in upon him.

Here is a charming example of a recantation in a letter to Mr. Burne-Jones :

"VENICE, 13*th May*, 1869.

"MY DEAREST NED,—There's nothing here like Carpaccio! There's a little bit of humble-pie for you !

"Well, the fact was, I had never once looked at him, having classed him in glance and thought with Gentile Bellini and other men of the more or less incipient and hard schools, and Tintoret went better with clouds and hills. But this Carpaccio is a new world to me. . . . I've only seen the Academy ones yet, and am going this morning (——— cloudless light) to your St. George of the Schiavoni ; but I must send this word first to catch post.

" From your loving　　　　　　　　　J. R.

"I don't give up my Tintoret, but his dissoluteness of expression into drapery and shadow is too licentious for me now."

It is to Watts I also owe the following letters, which are so interesting in themselves, and do such honor to the candor and love of truth of the recipients, that I will set them down without comment. The letters recall that past vision of Little Holland House and its gardens, where for many years Watts, "the Signor," as his friends all call him, dwelt on, recording the generation of noble people passing by, as well as the beautiful ideals of his own mind, working day after day quietly from dawn of light to afternoon in that home of so much vivid life and original color, which has left the remembrance of kind deeds and happy, gracious ways shining like a track on the waters.

"SATURDAY EVENING, 29th September, 1860.

"DEAR WATTS,—I am very glad to have your letter to-night, having been downhearted lately and unable to write to my friends, yet glad of being remembered by them. I have kept a kind letter of Mrs. Prinsep's by me ever so long. It came too late to be answered before the birthday of which it told me.

"I will come and sit whenever and wherever and as long as you like. I have nothing whatever to do, and don't mean to have. I hope to be at National Gallery on Tuesday [erased], Wednesday [erased ; see end of note], and Thursday afternoons, two to four, not exactly working, but wondering. I entirely feel with you that there is no dodge in Titian. It is simply right doing with a care and dexterity alike unpractised among us nowadays. It is drawing with paint as tenderly as you do with chalk. . . . I suspect that Titian depended on states and times in coloring more

115

than we do—that he left such and such colors for such and such times always before retouching, and so on ; but this you would not call dodge —would you ?—but merely perfect knowledge of means.   It struck me in looking at your group with child in the Academy that you depended too much on blending and too little on handling color ; that you were not simple enough nor quick enough to do all you felt ; nevertheless it was very beautiful.   I should think you were tormented a little by having too much feeling.

"If it is fine to - morrow I have promised to take a drive, but the *second* fine day, whatever that may be this week, I shall be at Trafalgar Square."

"MY DEAR WATTS,—Kind thanks for writing to ask for me.   I am not unwell materially, but furiously sulky and very quiet over my work, and mean to be so, and having been hitherto a rather voluble and dem- onstrative person, people think I'm ill.   I'm not cheerful, certainly, and don't see how anybody in their senses can be.

"I did not say—did I ?—that you were not to aim at all qualities ; but not all *at once*.   Titian was born of strong race, and with every con- ceivable human advantage, and probably before he was twelve years old knew all that could be done with oil-painting.   *We* are under every conceivable human disadvantage, and we must be content to go slowly. If you try at present to get all Titian's qualities, you will assuredly get none.   You not only *have* seen Titians and Correggios which united all, but I don't suppose you ever saw a true Titian or Correggio which did *not* unite all.   But that does not in the least warrant you in trying at once to do the same—you have many things to discover which they learned with their alphabet, many things to cure yourself of which their master never allowed them to fall into habit of.   For instance, from long drawing with chalk point you have got a mottled and broken execution, and have no power of properly modulating the brush.   Well, the way to cure yourself of that is not by trying for Titian or Correggio, whose modulations are so exquisite that they perpetually blend invisibly with the point-work, but take a piece of absolute modulation — the head of the kneeling figure in Sir Joshua's ' Three Graces ' at Kensington, for instance—and do it twenty times over and over again, restricting your- self wholly to his number of touches and thereabouts.   Then you will feel exactly where you are, and what is the obstacle in that direction to be vanquished ; you will feel progress every day, and be happy in it ; while when you try for everything, you never know what is stopping you. Again, the chalk drawing has materially damaged your perception of the subtlest qualities of local color. When a form is shown by a light of one color and a reflex of another, both equal in depth, if we are drawing in chalk we must exaggerate either one or the other, or the form must be invisible. The habit of exaggeration is fatal to the color vision; to conquer it you should paint the purest and subtlest colored objects on a small scale till you can realize them thoroughly. I say on a *small* scale ; otherwise the eye does not come to feel the value of points of hue. This exercise, nearly the reverse of the modulation exercise, could not be healthily carried on together with it. And so on with others.

"I write with an apparently presumptuous positiveness, but my own personal experience of every sort of feebleness is so great that I have a right to do so on points connected with it.

"Sincere regard to all friends.

"Ever affectionately yours, J. R."

"DENMARK HILL, S.,
"*Wednesday, 25th July*, 1866.

"MY DEAR WATTS,—I heard to-day from Edward * that he thought you would like to come and see me—or me to come to you.

"You have not been here for ever so long. Can you come out any day to breakfast ?—and we'll have a nice talk—or would you rather I should come in the afternoon ? I rarely stir in the morning. I want to see you. I've been very ill and sad lately, or should have managed it.

"Send me just a line to say what day you could come, or see me.

"Ever affectionately yours, J. RUSKIN.

"G. WATTS, Esq.

"Ned says you have been doing beautiful things. And therefore I should like to come, as you won't exhibit and leave Maclise's ' Death of Nelson ' to edify the public of taste, but I think you would enjoy *one* picture here."

And so, as one thinks of it all, of the people living round about us shaping their own and other people's lives, one admires and wonders at this unending variety of power and

* Mr. E. Burne-Jones.

117

voice of apprehension, of teaching, of opinion. Few things strike one more among the chief men who come to the front —not by chance, but by force of hard work and natural right—than their good-fellowship, their trust in one another, and their genuine appreciation of each other, whatever their opinions may be. It is more commonly the second rate among us who are critical and impatient. And this is indeed the secret of the rule of those Captains of our race who *are* Captains by reason of their swifter knowledge and insight, their greater courage and fairness.

We have all been reading lately of generous Darwin and his friends. Genuine excellence is distinguished by this mark, that it *belongs to all mankind*, says Goethe, writing to Carlyle. Carlyle himself, with his flashing wit and his passionate flashing words, discriminates even while he grumbles. Ruskin has *phases* of impression, but his noble instinct is for the truth, although the examples he gives at times seem so changeable, and his systems of instruction almost hopeless for students who have to live during their short lives; to pay their way and their long bills as well as to study their art. Ruskin's own peculiar system is in reality almost more of a trial of patience than of skill; he has a series of pitfalls for unwary students, among which the white jam pots he used to prescribe to those of Oxford may be counted. But though his practice may be fanciful, his light is a beacon indeed, steadily flashing from the rock upon which it is set. The rays fall upon uncertain waves, change their color, turn and return, dazzle or escape you altogether; but the longer you look at them, the more you realize their truth and their beauty. You can't take up a book with any one of the fanciful charming names, whether the *Queen of the Air*, or *Sesame and Lilies*, or the *Crown of Wild Olive*, that you don't find conscience and good common-sense wrapped up and hidden among the flowers. The shrewdness, the wisdom of it all strikes us as much as the variety of his interests.

"A few words," he says somewhere, "well chosen and well distinguished, will do work that a thousand cannot, when every one is acting equivocally in the function of another. Yes; and words, if they are not watched, will do deadly work sometimes, masked words—unjust stewards of men's ideas."

How true is this sentence concerning the idle and the busy: "All rich people are not idle. There are the idle rich and the idle poor, as there are the busy rich and the busy poor. Many a beggar is as lazy as if he had ten thousand a year; many a man of fortune is busier than his errand-boy."

Here is his definition of a true Church: "Wherever one hand meets another helpfully—that is the Holy or Mother Church which ever is or ever shall be."

About books: "Will you go and gossip with your house-maid or your stable-boy when you may talk with queens and kings? But we cannot read unless our minds are fit. Avarice, injustice, vulgarity, base excitement, all unfit us. Beware of reading in order to say, 'Thus Milton thought,' rather than, 'Thus I thought in misreading Milton.'"

Here is another hint respecting books for women: "Whether novels or history or poetry be read, they should be chosen not for what is *out* of them, but for what is *in* them. The chance and scattered evil that may here and there haunt and hide itself in a powerful book never does any harm to a noble girl, but the emptiness of an author oppresses her and his amiable folly degrades her." On education, as on the relations between men and women, he has a thousand delightful things to say. "Keep a fairy or two for your children," says kind Ruskin; and doubtless acting upon this friendly hint, the School Board has adopted that charming history of the *King of the Golden River* as a standard prize book.

It is pretty to read of the way in which Ruskin adjusts the different offices of the husband and the wife. The woman's a guiding, not a determining function. The man is the doer, the creator; the woman's power is for rule and not for battle. Her great function is *praise;* she enters into no contest, but adjudges the crown.

XIII

I am told by Mr. Allen that Mr. Ruskin thinks that the book which will stand the longest is the *Crown of Wild Olive.* *Sesame and Lilies* is, and most deservedly so, a favorite book with the public. Who can ever forget the closing passages, in which the poet, looking round about, seeing the need of the children even greater than that of their elders, bids women go forth into the garden and tend the flowerets lying broken, with their fresh leaves torn; set them in order in their little beds, fence them from the fierce wind — "flowers with eyes like yours, with thoughts like yours." Was ever a lesson more tenderly given?

How true is this description of Holman Hunt : "To Rossetti the Old and New Testaments were only the greatest poems he knew. But to Holman Hunt the story of the New Testament, when once his mind entirely fastened on it, became what it was to an old Puritan, . . . not merely a Reality, not merely the greatest of Realities, but the only Reality."

I have perhaps quoted too much already, but I cannot help giving a passage from the *Stones of Venice,* which is written in a different key, a very grave and noble one. He says: "The passions of mankind are partly protective, partly beneficent, like the chaff and grain of the corn, but none without their use, none without nobleness when seen in balanced unity with the rest of the spirit they are charged to defend. The passions of which the end is the continuance of the race, the indignation which is to arm it against injustice or strengthen it to resist wanton injury, and the fear which lies at the root of prudence, reverence, and awe, are all honorable and beautiful so long as man is regarded in his relations to the existing world."

Another lesson which Ruskin would impress upon us all is one more easy to grasp, and it applies to the whole conduct of life, whether in art, or in nature and natural phenomena. "The seed the sower sows grows up according to its kind : let us sow good seed with care and liberality." When Ruskin tells us that modesty, piety, humility, and a number of somewhat unexpected attributes are to be found in the curl of a leaf, in the painted background of a picture, or in the arch of a window, a moment's thought will show how true his words are. Qualities take different forms in their exercise : Modesty in design would mean care and accuracy; Humility would mean interest in the object copied, not a vulgar desire for self-glorification and for rapid effect ; Piety represents that sweet sense which some call sentiment.

Then again listen to Ruskin writing upon a different theme, that of Shakespeare's chivalry. "Note broadly in the outset that Shakespeare has no heroes, whereas there is hardly a play that has not a perfect woman in it, steadfast in grave . hope and errorless purpose. Cordelia, Desdemona, Isabella, Hermione, Imogen, Queen Katherine, Perdita, Sylvia, Viola, Rosalind, Helena, and last and perhaps loveliest, Virgilia, are all faultless, conceived in the highest

heroic type of humanity. Then observe, secondly, the catastrophe of every play is caused always by the folly or
fault of a man ; the redemption, if there be any, is by the
wisdom or virtue of a woman."

One of Shakespeare's heroines (a Helen happily belonging to our own time) has dedicated to Ruskin one of her
charming renderings of her not forgotten parts. "She"
(Lady Martin) "has shown her beautiful sympathy with
character in choosing Beatrice," Ruskin writes in return to
Sir Theodore Martin, "and she may be assured that I am
indeed listening with all my heart to every word she will
say." And then again to Lady Martin herself: "I thought
I knew Beatrice of any lady by heart, but you have made
her still more real and dear to me, especially by the little
sentences in which you speak of your own feelings in certain moments in acting her. You have made me wretched
because Beatrice is not at Brantwood." . . . "I should like
a pomegranate or two in Juliet's balcony," he adds. I take
up another letter to Sir Theodore Martin at hazard, and
read : "You are happy at Llangollen in this season. The
ferns and grass of its hills are far more beautifully and softly opposed than on ours." How few of us know how to
think with such vividness! — we think of a valley, of a
mountain, of the skies beyond it, but we don't instinctively
see the details ; we don't contrast the hue of the ferns and
of the turf of Cumberland and of Wales, perceiving it all
with that instantaneous conception which is genius, in
short.

I once heard a well-known man of science speaking of
Ruskin ; some one had asked him whether Ruskin or Goethe
had done most for science. Sir John Lubbock replied that
Ruskin undoubtedly had done very much more valuable
work than Goethe ; and that without any pretensions to
profound scientific knowledge, he had an extraordinary

natural gift for observation, and seemed to know by instinct *what* to observe, what was important amid so much that was fanciful and poetical; and then he went on to quote the description of the swallow from *Love's Meinie*, one of the loveliest things imaginable, and which it would not be difficult to apply to Ruskin's own genius—so swift, so unerring in its flight, so incalculable, so harmonious and fascinating always.

Mr. Ruskin is a figure standing out distinguished among the many figures and characters which make up the *dramatis personæ* of our time; and this being so, legends gather round him as clouds gather round the peak of his own Coniston Old Man. One story I have vaguely heard which describes a Haroun-al-Raschid expedition of his through the streets of London, a flight from the mosque to the jeweller's store, where the loveliest gems are heaped before him, of which he can best tell the secrets. Then from the jeweller's store to the pastry-cook's, where in an inner room a table is spread, not with the cream tarts of fiction, but with the British fare of roast mutton and potatoes, and where, as the poet lunches, salting his food meanwhile with his enchanting talk, little by little all the people already in the shop leaving their buns and sandwiches, gather round to listen. Another legend, which I cannot vouch for either, but which seems suitable somehow, begins with a dream, in which Ruskin dreamt himself a Franciscan friar. Now I am told that when he was at Rome there was a beggar on the steps of the Pincio who begged of Mr. Ruskin every day as he passed, and who always received something. On one occasion the grateful beggar suddenly caught the out-stretched hand and kissed it. Mr. Ruskin stopped short, drew his hand hastily away, and then, with a sudden impulse, bending forward, kissed the beggar's cheek. The next day the man came to Mr. Ruskin's lodging to find him, bringing a gift, which he offered with tears in his eyes. It was a relic, he said, a shred of brown cloth which had once formed part of the robe of St. Francis. Mr. Ruskin remembered his dream when the poor beggar brought forth his relic, and thence, so I am told, came his pilgrimage to the convent of St. Francis Assisi, where he beheld those frescos by Giotto which seemed to him more lovely than anything Tintoret himself had ever produced. I personally should like to believe that the mendicant was St. Francis appearing in the garb of a beggar to his great disciple, to whom also had been granted the gift of interpreting the voice of Nature.

We are all apt to feel at times that meat is more than life, and the raiment more than the soul; at such times let us turn to Ruskin. He sees the glorious world as we have never known it, or have perhaps forgotten to look upon it. He takes the first example to hand; the stones, which he makes into bread; the dust and scraps and dry sticks and moss which are lying to his hand; he is so penetrated with the glory and beauty of it all, of the harmony into which we are set, that it signifies little to him upon what subject he preaches, and by what examples he illustrates his meaning; there is a blessing upon his words, and surely the fragments which remain are worthy of the twelve baskets of the Apostles.

It seemed to me one day last summer as if in truth Ruskin's actual page was shining before me as I waited on the slope of Blackdown Moor in Surrey. It was the day of the Naval Review, and as I rested in a blackberry-bordered field I could see the tossing land-waves alive with summer and summer toil, the laborers patiently pacing and repacing the furrows, the hay-carts unloading; other hedges again dividing harvest from harvest, labor from labor; and in the far distance a dazzling plain, with gleams of white like the breakers of the sea, and overhead a midsummer vault of blue, across which a hawk was darting in glorious serenity. One of Ruskin's books was lying open on the grass, and the very page seemed to slide forth to fill the air; now and then a faint breeze would shake the leaves and the countless points and blossoms upon the trees and hedges still in my Ruskin land round about; while from time to time could be heard the distant echo of the Portsmouth guns saluting the Queen as she passed among her ships.

NOTE.—This note is from the *Pall Mall Gazette* of March 28, 1887, and was compiled from information given by Mr. Allen, to show what the comparative sale of Mr. Ruskin's books had been for 1886:

Sesame and Lilies (small edition), 2122; Frondes Agrestes, 1273; Stones of Venice (large edition), 939; Unto this Last, 874; Ethics of the Dust, 808; Fors Clavigera (volumes of), 730; Seven Lamps of Architecture, 668; Modern Painters, Vol. II. (small edition), 652; Stones of Venice (small travellers' edition, in two vols.), each, 675; On the Old Road, 597; King of the Golden River, 388.

Of the books issuing in parts, the following figures will be interesting:

Præterita (20 parts issued), 63,386; The Art of England (7 parts issued), 1929; Road-side Songs of Tuscany (10 parts issued), 1459; Proserpina, 921.

The *King of the Golden River*, it may be interesting to add, is largely bought by the London School Board for prizes. Mr. Ruskin's *Letter to Young Girls* has also a large sale, 264 packets (containing 3168 copies in all) having been sold during last year.

With regard to the "Revised Series" of Mr. Ruskin's works, the following were the sales during 1886:

Sesame and Lilies, 272; Crown of Wild Olive, 188; Queen of the Air, 108; Eagle's Nest, 104; Two Paths, 96; Time and Tide, 89; Munera Pulveris, 73; *Val d'Arno, 54; *Aratra Pentelice, 53; A Joy Forever, 51; *Ariadne Florentina, 40.

This series, it should be stated, is a very expensive one, the ordinary volumes costing 13s. each (unbound), the illustrated (marked above with an asterisk), 22s. 6d. The unillustrated volumes are, however, all in course of being issued in cheap form, similar to the small *Sesame and Lilies*, of which over 2000 copies were sold last year. *Præterita* is steadily increasing in popularity. Last year 3169 copies of each part were sold on an average. Mr. Allen is now printing for first edition 5000 copies of each.

ROBERT AND ELIZABETH BARRETT BROWNING

I

THE sons and daughters of men and women eminent in their generation are from circumstances fortunate in their opportunities. From childhood they know their parents' friends and contemporaries, the remarkable men and women who are the makers of the age, quite naturally and without excitement. At the same time this facility may perhaps detract in some degree from the undeniable glamour of the Unknown, and, indeed, it is not till much later in life that the time comes to appreciate.

B or C or D are great men; we know it because our fathers have told us; but the moment when we *feel* it for ourselves comes suddenly and mysteriously. My own experience certainly is this: the friends existed first; then, long afterwards, they became to me the notabilities, the interesting people as well, and these two impressions were oddly combined in my mind. When we were children living in Paris, we used to look with a certain mingled terror and fascination at various pages of grim heads drawn in black and red chalk, something in the manner of Fuseli. Masks and faces were depicted, crowding together with malevolent or agonized or terrific expressions. There were the suggestions of a hundred weird stories on the pages at which one gazed with creeping alarm. These pictures were all drawn by a kind and most gentle neighbor of ours, whom we all often met and visited, and of whom we were not in the very least afraid. His name was Mr. Robert Browning. He was the father of the poet, and he lived with his daughter in calm and pleasant retreat in those Champs-Elysées to which so many people used to come at that time seeking well-earned repose from their labors by crossing the Channel instead of the Styx. I don't know whether Mr. and Miss Browning always lived in Paris; they are certainly among the people I can longest recall there. But one day I found myself listening with some interest to a conversation which had been going on for some time between my grandparents and Miss Browning—a long matter-of-fact talk about houses, travellers, furnished apartments, sunshine, south aspects, etc., and on asking who were the travellers coming to inhabit the apartments, I was told that our Mr. Browning had a son who lived abroad, and who was expected shortly with his wife from Italy, and that the rooms were to be engaged for them; and I was also told that they were very gifted and celebrated people; and I further remember that very afternoon being taken over various vacant houses and lodgings by my grandmother. Mrs. Browning was an invalid, my grandmother told me, who could not possibly live without light and warmth. So that by the time the travellers had really arrived, and were definitively installed, we were all greatly excited and interested in their whereabouts, and well convinced that wherever else the sun might or might not fall, it must shine upon *them*. In this homely fashion the shell of the future—the four walls of a friendship—began to exist before the friends themselves walked into it. We were taken to call very soon after they arrived. Mr. Browning was not there, but Mrs. Browning received us in a low room with Napoleonic chairs and tables, and a wood-fire burning on the hearth.

I don't think any girl who had once experienced it could fail to respond to Mrs. Browning's motherly advance. There was something more than kindness in it; there was an implied interest, equality, and understanding which is very difficult to describe and impossible to forget. This generous humility of nature was also to the last one special attribute of Robert Browning himself, translated by him into cheerful and vigorous good-will and utter absence of affectation. But again and again one is struck by that form of greatness which consists in reaching the reality in all things, instead of keeping to the formalities and the affectations of life. The free-and-easiness of the small is a very different thing from this. It may be as false in its way as formality itself, if it is founded on conditions which do not and can never exist.

To the writer's own particular taste there never will be any more delightful person than the simple-minded woman of the world, who has seen enough to know what its praise is all worth, who is sure enough of her own position to take it for granted, who is interested in the person she is talking to, and unconscious of anything but a wish to give kindness and attention. This is the impression Mrs. Browning made upon me from the first moment I ever saw her to the last. Alas! the moments were not so very many when we were together. Perhaps all the more vivid is the recollection of the peaceful home, of the fireside where the logs are burning while the lady of that kind hearth is established in her sofa corner, with her little boy curled up by her side, the door opening and shutting meanwhile to the quick step of the master of the house, to the life of the world without as it came to find her in her quiet nook. The hours seemed to my sister and to me warmer, more full of interest and peace, in her sitting-room than elsewhere. Whether at Florence, at Rome, at Paris, or in London once more, she seemed to carry her own atmosphere always, something serious, motherly, absolutely artless, and yet impassioned, noble, and sincere. I can recall the slight figure in its thin black dress, the writing apparatus by the sofa, the tiny inkstand, the quill-nibbed pen—the unpretentious implements of her magic. "She was a little woman; she liked little things," Mr. Browning used to say. Her miniature editions of the classics are still carefully preserved, with her name written in each in her delicate, sensitive handwriting, and always with her husband's name above her own, for she dedicated all her books to him; it was a fancy that she had. Nor must his presence in the home be forgotten any more than in the books—the spirited domination and inspired common-sense, which seemed to give a certain life to her vaguer visions. But of these visions Mrs. Browning rarely spoke; she was too simple and practical to indulge in many apostrophes.

II

To all of us who have only known Mrs. Browning in her own home as a wife and a mother, it seems almost impossible to realize the time before her home existed—when Mrs. Browning was *not*, and Elizabeth Barrett, dwelling apart, was weaving her spells like the Lady of Shalott, and subject, like the lady herself, to the visions in her mirror.

Mrs. Browning* was born in the County of Durham, on the 6th of March, 1809. It was a golden year for poets, for it was also that of Tennyson's birth. She was the eldest daughter of Edward Moulton, and was christened by the names of Elizabeth Barrett. Not long after her birth Mr. Moulton, succeeded to some property, and took the name of Barrett, so that in after-times, when Mrs. Browning signed

* The passages relating to Mrs. Browning's life are taken (by the permission of the proprietor and editor) from an article contributed by the present writer to the "Biographical Dictionary" published by Messrs. Smith, Elder & Co.

ELIZABETH BARRETT BROWNING

herself at length as Elizabeth Barrett Browning, it was her own Christian name that she used without any further literary assumptions. Her mother was Mary Graham, the daughter of a Mr. Graham, afterwards known as Mr. Graham Clark, of Northumberland. Soon after the child's birth her parents brought her southward, to Hope End, near Ledbury, in Herefordshire, where Mr. Barrett possessed a considerable estate, and had built himself a country-house. The house is now pulled down, but it is described by Lady Carmichael, one of the family, as "a luxurious home standing in a lovely park, among trees and sloping hills all sprinkled with sheep;" and this same lady remembers the great hall, with the great organ in it, and more especially Elizabeth's room, a lofty chamber, with a stained-glass window casting lights across the floor, and little Elizabeth as she used to sit propped against the wall, with her hair falling all about her face. There were gardens round about the house leading to the park. Most of the children had their own plots to cultivate, and Elizabeth was famed among them all for success with her white roses. She had a bower of her own all overgrown with them; it is still blooming for the readers of the lost bower "as once beneath the sunshine." Another favorite device with the child was that of a man of flowers, laid out in beds upon the lawn—a huge giant wrought of blossom. "Eyes of gentianella azure, staring, winking at the skies."

Mr. Barrett was a rich man, and his daughter's life was that of a rich man's child, far removed from the stress and also from the variety and experience of humbler life; but her eager spirit found adventure for itself. Her gift for learning was extraordinary. At eight years old little Elizabeth had a tutor and could read Homer in the original, holding her book in one hand and nursing her doll on the other arm. She has said herself that in those days "the

Greeks were her demi-gods; she dreamed more of Agamemnon than of Moses, her black pony." At the same small age she began to try her childish powers. When she was about eleven or twelve, her great epic of the battle of Marathon was written in four books, and her proud father had it printed. "Papa was bent upon spoiling me," she writes. Her cousin remembers a certain ode the little girl recited to her father on his birthday; as he listened, shading his eyes, the young cousin was wondering why the tears came falling along his cheek. It seems right to add on this same authority that their common grandmother, who used to stay at the house, did not approve of these readings and writings, and said she had far rather see Elizabeth's hemming more carefully finished off than hear of all this Greek.

Elizabeth was growing up meanwhile under happy influences; she had brothers and sisters in her home; her life was not all study; she had the best of company—that of happy children as well as of all natural things; she loved her hills, her gardens, her woodland play-ground. As she grew older she used to drive a pony and go farther afield. There is a story still told of a little child, flying in terror along one of the steep Herefordshire lanes, perhaps frightened by a cow's horn beyond the hedge, who was overtaken by a young girl, with a pale, spiritual face and a profusion of dark curls, driving a pony-carriage, and suddenly caught up into safety and driven rapidly away. But, alas! it was very early in her life that Elizabeth's happy drives and rides were discontinued, and the sad apprenticeship to suffering began. Was it Moses, the black pony, who was so nearly the cause of her death? One day, when she was about fifteen, the young girl, impatient to get out, tried to saddle her pony in a field alone, and fell, with the saddle upon her, in some way injuring her spine so seriously that she lay for years upon her back.

She was about twenty when her mother's last illness began, and at the same time some money catastrophe, the result of other people's misdeeds, overtook Mr. Barrett. He would not allow his wife to be troubled or to be told of this crisis in his affairs, and he compounded with his creditors at an enormous cost, materially diminishing his income for life, so as to put off any change in the ways at Hope End until change could trouble the sick lady no more. After her death, when Elizabeth was a little over twenty, they came away, leaving Hope End among the hills forever. "Beautiful, beautiful hills!" Miss Barrett wrote long after from her closed sick-room in London, "and yet not for the whole world's beauty would I stand among the sunshine and shadow of them any more. It would be a mockery, like the taking back a broken flower to its stalk."

The family spent two years at Sidmouth, and afterwards came to London, where Mr. Barrett first bought a house in Gloucester Place, and then removed to Wimpole Street. His daughter's continued delicacy and failure of health kept her for months at a time a prisoner to her room, but did not prevent her from living her own life of eager and beautiful aspiration. She was becoming known to the world. Her *Prometheus*, which was published when she was twenty-six years old, was reviewed in the *Quarterly Review* for 1840, and there Miss Barrett's name comes second among a list of the most accomplished women of those days, whose little tinkling guitars are scarcely audible now, while this one voice vibrates only more clearly as the echoes of her time die away.

Her noble poem on "Cowper's Grave" was republished with the "Seraphim,"* by which (whatever her later opinion may have been) she seems to have set small count at the

* In a surviving copy of this book, belonging to Mr. Dykes Campbell, there is an added stanza to the "Image of God" never yet printed, and also many corrections in her delicate handwriting.

time, "all the remaining copies of the book being locked away in the wardrobe in her father's bedroom," "entombed as safely as Œdipus among the Olives."

From Wimpole Street Miss Barrett went, an unwilling exile for her health's sake, to Torquay, where the tragedy occurred which, as she writes to Mr. Horne, "gave a nightmare to her life forever." Her companion-brother had come to see her and to be with her and to be comforted by her for some trouble of his own, when he was accidentally drowned, under circumstances of suspense which added to the shock. All that year the sea beating upon the shore sounded to her as a dirge, she says in a letter to Miss Mitford. It was long before Miss Barrett's health was sufficiently restored to allow of her being brought home to Wimpole Street, where many years passed away in confinement to a sick-room, to which few besides members of her own family were admitted. Among these exceptions was her devoted Miss Mitford, who would "travel forty miles to see her for an hour." Besides Miss Mitford, Mrs. Jameson also came, and, above all, Mr. Kenyon, the friend and dearest cousin, to whom Mrs. Browning afterwards dedicated *Aurora Leigh*. Mr. Kenyon had an almost fatherly affection for her, and from the first recognized his young relative's genius. He was a constant visitor and her link with the outside world, and he never failed to urge her to write, and to live out and beyond the walls of her chamber.

Miss Barrett lay on her couch with her dog Flush at her feet, and Miss Mitford describes her reading every book, in almost every language, and giving herself heart and soul to poetry. She also occupied herself with prose, writing literary articles for the *Athenæum*, and contributing to a modern rendering of Chaucer, which was then being edited by her unknown friend, Mr. R. H. Horne, from whose correspondence with her I have already quoted, and whose interest in literature and occupation with literary things must have brought wholesome distractions to the monotonies of her life.

The early letters of Mrs. Browning to Mr. Horne, written before her marriage, and published with her husband's sanction after her death, are full of the suggestions of her delightful fancy. Take, for instance, " Sappho, who broke off a fragment of her soul for us to guess at." Of herself she says (apparently in answer to some questions), " My story amounts to the knife-grinder's, with nothing at all for a catastrophe ! *A bird in a cage would have as good a story; most of my events and nearly all my intense pleasures have passed in my thoughts.*" But such a woman, though living so quietly and thus secluded from the world, could not have been altogether out of touch with its changing impressions. Here is an instance of her unconscious presence in the minds of others: "I remember all those sad circumstances connected with the last doings of poor Haydon." Mr. Browning writes to Professor Knight, in 1882 : " He never saw my wife, but interchanged letters with her occasionally. On visiting her, the day before the painter's death, I found her room occupied by a quantity of studies—sketches and portraits—which, together with paints, palettes, and brushes, he had chosen to send, in apprehension of an arrest or, at all events, an 'execution' in his own house. The letter which apprised her of this step said, in excuse of it, 'they may have a right to my goods; they can have none to my mere work tools and necessaries of existence,' or words to that effect. The next morning I read the account in the *Times*, and myself hastened to break the news at Wimpole Street, but had been anticipated. Every article was at once sent back, no doubt. I do not remember noticing Wordsworth's portrait—it never belonged to my wife, certainly, at any time. She possessed an engraving of the head ; I suppose a gift from poor Haydon. . . ."

WHEN Mrs. Orr's authoritative history of Robert Browning appeared, the writer felt that it was but waste of time to attempt anything like a biographical record. Hers is but a personal record of impressions and remembrances. Others, with more knowledge of his early days, have described Robert Browning as a child, as a boy, and a very young man. How interesting, among other things, is the account of the little child among his animals and pets; and of the tender mother taking so much pains to find the original editions of Shelley and of Keats, and giving them to her boy at a time when their works were scarcely to be bought!* Browning was a year younger than my own father, and was born at Camberwell, in May, 1812. He went to Italy when he was twenty years of age, and there he studied hard, laying in a noble treasury of facts and fancies to be dealt out in after-life, when the time comes to draw upon the past, upon that youth which age spends so liberally, and which is "the background of pale gold" upon which all our lives are painted.

Browning's first published poem was "Pauline," coming out in 1833, the same year as the "Miller's Daughter" and the "Dream of Fair Women." And we are also told that

---

* There is a little story in Mrs. Orr's book which Mr. Browning himself once told some of the children of our family: how, when he was a small boy at school, there was one solemn day in the week when all the little scholars' hairs were brushed and rubbed with oil, which was the fashion in those days, while their mistress chanted Watts's hymns to them, especially that one which begins "Anoint with heavenly grace."

ROBERT BROWNING

From a copyrighted photograph by W. H. Grove, 174 Brompton Road, London

Dante Rossetti, then a very young man, admired "Pauline" so much that he copied * the whole poem out from the book in the British Museum.

In 1834 Robert Browning went to Russia, and there wrote "Porphyria's Lover," published by Mr. Fox in a Unitarian magazine, where the poem must have looked somewhat out of place. It was at Mr. Fox's house that Browning first met Macready.

Notwithstanding many differences and consequent estrangements, I have often heard Mr. Browning speak of the great actor with interest and sympathy; the last time being when *Recollections of Macready*, a book by Lady Pollock, had just come out. She had sent Mr. Browning a copy, with which he was delighted. He said he had stopped at home all that winter's day reading it by the fire, and now that dinner-time was come he could quote page after page from memory. His memory was to the last most remarkable.

There is a touching passage in Mrs. Orr's book describing the meeting of Browning and Macready after their long years of estrangement. Both had seen their homes wrecked and desolate; both had passed through deep waters. They met unexpectedly and grasped each other's hands again. "Oh! Macready," said Browning. And neither of them could speak another word.

I have been fortunate for years past in being able to count upon the help of a recording friend and neighbor, to whom I sometimes go for the magic of a suggestive touch when together we conjure up things out of the past.

I wrote to ask Lady Martin about the production of Mr. Browning's plays upon the stage, and she sent me the following account of her recollections of "Strafford;" nor can

* The writer has in her possession a book in which her own father, somewhere about those same years, copied out Tennyson's "Day Dream" verse by verse.

I do better now than insert her answer here at length, for to cut out any word is to destroy the impression which it gives:

"*April* 30, 1891, BRIGHTON.

"The production of Browning's 'Strafford,' which you ask me about, occurred so early in my career that anything I could say about it would be, I fear, of little use to you. I was so young then, and just a mere novice in my art, so that my first feeling, when I heard the play read, was one of wonder that such a weighty character as Lucy, Countess of Carlisle, should be intrusted to my hands. I was told that Mr. Browning had particularly wished me to undertake it. I naturally felt the compliment implied in the wish, but this only increased my surprise, which did not diminish as I advanced in the study of the character.

"Lady Carlisle, as drawn by Mr. Browning, a woman versed in all the political struggles and intrigues of the times, did not move me. The only interest she awoke in me was due to her silent love for Strafford and devotion to his cause; and I wondered why, depending so absolutely as he did upon her sympathy, her intelligence, her complete self-abnegation, he should only have, in the early part, a common expression of gratitude to give her in return.

"This made the treatment of Lucy's character, as you will readily see, all the more difficult in the necessity it imposed upon me of letting her feeling be seen by the audience, without its being perceptible to Strafford.

"Of course I did my best to carry out what I conceived was Mr. Browning's view; and he, at all events, I had reason to know, was well satisfied with my efforts. I had met him at Mr. and Mrs. Macready's house previously, so that at the rehearsals we renewed our acquaintance.

"I suppose he was nervous, for I remember Mr. Macready read the play to us in the greenroom. And how finely he read! He made the smallest part distinct and prominent. He was accused of under-reading his own part. But I do not think this was so.

"At the rehearsals, when Mr. Browning was introduced to those ladies and gentlemen whom he did not know, his demeanor was so kind, considerate, and courteous, so grateful for the attention shown to his wishes, that he won directly the warm interest of all engaged in the play. So it was that although many doubtful forecasts were made in the greenroom as to the ultimate attraction of a play so entirely turning on politics, yet all were determined to do their very best to insure its success.

"In the play Lucy has only to meet Strafford, King Charles, and Henrietta. It seemed to me that Mr. Macready's Strafford was a fine performance. The character fitted in with his restless, nervous, changeable, impetuous, and emphatic style. He looked the very man as we knew him in Vandyck's famous picture. The royal personages were very feebly represented. I could not help feeling in the scenes with them that my earnestness was overdone, and that I had no business to appear to dominate and sway and direct opinions while they stood nerveless by.

"There were some fine moments in the play. The last scene must have been very exciting and touching. Lucy believes that by her means Strafford's escape is certain ; but when the water-gates open, with the boat ready to receive him, *Pym steps out of it!* . . . This effect was most powerful.

"It was a dreadful moment. My heart seemed to cease to beat. I sank on my knees, burying my head in my bosom, and stopping my ears with my hands while the death-bell tolled for Strafford.

"I can remember nothing more than that I went home very sad ; for although the play was considered a success, yet, somehow, even my small experience seemed to tell me it would not be a very long life, and that perhaps kind Mr. Browning would think we had not done our best for him.

"The play was mounted in all matters with great care. Modern critics seem to have little knowledge of the infinite pains bestowed in all respects before their day upon the representation of historical and Shakespearian *plays* and noteworthy *people* in romance or history.

"I can see my gown now in Lucy Percy, made from a Vandyck picture, and remember the thought bestowed even upon the *kind* of fur with which the gown was trimmed. The same minute attention to accuracy of costume prevailed in all the characters produced. The scenery was alike accurate, if not so full of small details as at present. The *human beings* dominated all."

I need scarcely add that I have heard from others of Miss Helen Faucit's perfect rendering of the part of Lucy Carlisle. Browning himself spoke of Miss Faucit's "playing as an actress, and her perfect behavior as a woman."

IV

My friend, Professor Knight, has kindly given me leave to quote from some of his interesting letters from Robert Browning. One most interesting record describes the poet's own first acquaintance with Mr. Kenyon. The letter is dated January the 10th, 1884, but the events related, of course, to some forty years before:

"With respect to the information you desire about Mr. Kenyon, all that I do 'know of him — better than anybody,' perhaps — is his great goodness to myself. Singularly, little respecting his early life came to my knowledge. He was the cousin of Mr. Barrett; second cousin, therefore, of my wife, to whom he was ever deeply attached. I first met him at a dinner of Sergeant Talfourd's, after which he drew his chair by mine and inquired whether my father had been his old school-fellow and friend at Cheshunt, adding that, in a poem just printed, he had been commemorating their play-ground fights, armed with sword and shield, as Achilles and Hector, some half-century before. On telling this to my father at breakfast, next morning, he at once, with a pencil, sketched me the boy's handsome face, still distinguishable in the elderly gentleman's I had made acquaintance with. Mr. Kenyon at once renewed his own acquaintance with my father, and became my fast friend; hence my introduction to Miss Barrett.

"He was one of the best of human beings, with a general sympathy for excellence of every kind. He enjoyed the friendship of Wordsworth, of Southey, of Landor; and, in later days, was intimate with most of my own contemporaries of eminence. I believe that he was born in the West Indies, whence his property was derived, as was that of Mr. Barrett, persistently styled a 'merchant' by biographers who will not take the pains to do more than copy the blunders of their forerunners in the business of article-mongery. He was twice married, but left no family. I should suggest Mr. Scharf (of the National Portrait Gallery) as a far more qualified informant on all such matters; my own concern having mainly been with his exceeding goodness to me and mine."

Mr. Kenyon has sometimes dined with my father. I can remember him, and also a smooth, fair printed book of his poems, with broad margins, and some odd suggestive look of its author. For many years he lived in Regent's Park. After his death, Mrs. Bayne, a kind and hospitable cousin of my father's, dwelt in the house with her daughter, who still resides there. My father used to say that the dining-room was the prettiest room in all London. It has wide green windows looking across the park, and there were grace-ful pillars to support the bay. As I sat at the round-table I used to hear of Mr. Kenyon's gatherings and the friends who met in the pretty sunny room where his picture still hangs, and where so many of his guests returned at the summons of their kind hostess. I remember my father sitting there and talking of the past, with affectionate words of remembrance, and Mr. Browning used to be often present with another of Mrs. Bayne's old friends, Dr. Connop Thirlwall; and as one thinks of it all, one feels, perhaps, that to remember old friends in peaceful festive hours is better for our souls than all the *memento mori* that ever were set up by perverse mor-tals struggling in vain against the repeated benedictions of Providence.

As we all know, it was Mr. Kenyon who first introduced Robert Browning to his future wife; and the story, as told by Mrs. Orr, is most romantic. The poet was about thirty-two years of age at this time, in the fulness of his powers. She was supposed to be a confirmed invalid, con-fined to her own room and to her couch, seeing no one, living her own spiritual life indeed, but looking for none other, when her cousin first brought Mr. Browning to the house. Miss Barrett's reputation was well established by this time. "Lady Geraldine's Courtship" was already published, in which the author had written of Browning, among other poets, as of "some pomegranate, which, if cut deep down the middle, shows a heart within blood-tinctured, of a veined humanity;" and one can well believe that this present meeting must have been but a phase in an old and long-existing sympathy between kindred spirits. Very soon afterwards the two became engaged, and they were married at Mary-le-Bone* Parish Church in the autumn of the year 1846.

Who does not know the story of this marriage of true souls? Has not Mrs. Browning herself spoken of it in words indelible and never to be quoted without sympathy by all women; while *he* from his own fireside has struck chord after chord of manly feeling than which this life contains nothing deeper or more true.

The Sonnets from the Portuguese were written by Elizabeth Barrett to Mr. Browning before her marriage, although she never even showed them to him till some years after they were man and wife. They were sonnets such as no Portuguese ever wrote before, or ever will write again. There is a quality in them which is beyond words, that echo which belongs to the highest human expression of feeling. But such a love to such a woman comes with its own Testament.

Some years before her marriage the doctors had positively declared that Miss Barrett's life depended upon her leaving England for the winter, and immediately after their marriage Mr. Browning took his wife abroad.

Mrs. Jameson was at Paris when Mr. and Mrs. Browning arrived there. There is an interesting account of the meet-

* See Biographical Dictionary.

ing, and of their all journeying together southward by Avignon and Vaucluse.* Can this be the life-long invalid of whom we read, perching out-of-doors upon a rock, among the shallow, curling waters of a stream? They come to a rest at Pisa, whence Mrs. Browning writes to her old friend, Mr. Horne, to tell him of her marriage, adding that Mrs. Jameson calls her, notwithstanding all the emotion and fatigue of the last six weeks, rather "transformed" than improved. From Pisa the new-married pair went to Florence, where they finally settled, and where their boy was born in 1849.

Poets are painters in words, and the color and the atmosphere of the country to which they belong seem to be repeated almost unconsciously in their work and its setting. Mrs. Browning was an Englishwoman; though she lived in Italy, though she died in Florence, though she loved the land of her adoption, yet she never, for all that, ceased to breathe her native air, as she sat by the Casa Guidi windows; and though Italian sunshine dazzled her dark eyes, and Italian voices echoed in the street, though her very ink was mixed with the waters of the Arno, she still wrote of Herefordshire lakes and hills, of the green land where "jocund childhood" played "dimpled close with hills and valley, dappled very close with shade." . . . Now that the writer has seen the first home and the last home of that kind friend of her girlhood, it seems to her as if she could better listen to that poet's song growing sweeter, as all true music does, with years.

We had been spending an autumn month in Mrs. Browning's country when we drove to visit the scene of her early youth, and it seemed to me as if an echo of her melody was still vibrating from hedge-row to hedge-row, even though the

* *Life of Mrs. Jameson*, by Mrs. Macpherson.

birds were silent, and though summer and singing-time were over. We drove along, my little son and I, towards Hope End, by a road descending gradually from the range of the Malvern Hills into the valley—it ran across commons sprinkled with geese and with lively donkeys, and skirted by the cottages still alight with sunflowers and nasturtium beds, for they were sheltered from the cold wind by the range of purple hills "looming a-row;" then we dipped into lanes between high banks heaped with ferns and leaves of every shade of burnished gold and brown, fenced up by the twisting roots of the chestnuts and oak-trees; and all along the way, as our old white horse jogged steadily on, we could see the briers and the blackberry sprays travelling too, advancing from tree to tree and from hedge to hedge, flashing their long flaming brands and warning tokens of winter's approaching armies. The wind was cold and in the north, the sky overhead was broken and stormy. Sometimes we dived into sudden glooms among rocks overhung with ivy and thick brushwood; then we came out into the open again, and caught sight of vast skies dashed with strange lights, a wonderful cloud-capped country up above, where the storm-clouds reared their vast piles out of sapphire depths —

> . . . "a boundless depth
> Far sinking into splendor without end."

Our adventures were not along the road, but chiefly overhead. My boy amused himself by counting the broken rainbows and the hail-storms falling in the distance; and then at last, just as we were getting cold and tired, we turned into the lodge gates of Hope End.

I don't know how the park strikes other people; to me, who paid this one short visit, it seemed a sort of enchanted garden revealed for an hour, and I almost expected that it

MRS. BROWNING'S TOMB AT FLORENCE

would then vanish away.* Everything was wild, abrupt, and yet suddenly harmonious. We passed an unsuspected lake covered with water-lilies. A flock of sheep at full gallop plunged across the road ; then came ponies, with long manes and round, wondering eyes, trotting after us. Sometimes in the Alps one has met such herds, wild creatures, sympathetic, not yet afraid! Finally we caught sight of the river,

* "Here's the garden she walked across . . .
   Down this side of the gravel walk
   She went while her robe's edge brushed the box :
   And here she paused in her gracious talk
   To point me a moth on the milk-white flox.
   Roses ranged in valiant row
   I will never think she passed you by :". . .
                                   Garden Fancies, R. B.

where a couple of water-fowl were flying into the sedges. But where was the wild swan's nest, and why was not the great god Pan there blowing upon his reed? It all seemed so natural and so vivid that I should not have been startled to see him sitting quietly by the side of the river.

V

THE only memoranda I ever made of Mrs. Browning's talk was when I was quite a young girl keeping a diary, and I heard her saying that Tennyson's Maud was "splendid;" and "that without illness she saw no reason why the mind should ever fail." The visitor to whom she expressed this opinion seems to have come away with me complaining that the conversation had been too matter-of-fact, too much to the point; nothing romantic, nothing poetic, such as one might expect from a poet! Another person also present had answered that was just the reason of Mrs. Browning's power—she kept her poetry for her poetry, and didn't scatter it about in conversation where it was not wanted; and then follows a girlish note in the old diary: "I think Mrs. Browning is the greatest woman I ever saw in all my life. She is very small, she is brown, with dark eyes and dead brown hair; she has white teeth, and a low, curious voice; she has a manner full of charm and kindness; she rarely laughs, but is always cheerful and smiling; her eyes are very bright. Her husband is not unlike her. He is short; he is dark, with a frank, open countenance, long hair, streaked with gray; he opens his mouth wide when he speaks; he has white teeth;" and there the diary wanders off.

When I first remember Mr. Browning he was a comparatively young man—though, for the matter of that, he was always young, as his father had been before him—and he was also happy in this, that the length of his life can best be measured by his work. In those days I had not read one single word of his poetry, but somehow one realized that it was there. Almost the first time I ever really recall Mr. Browning, he and my father and Mrs. Browning* were discussing spiritualism in a very human and material fashion, each holding to their own point of view, and my sister and I sat by listening and silent. My father was always immensely interested by the stories told of Spiritualism and table-turning, though he certainly scarcely believed half of them. Mrs. Browning believed, and Mr. Browning was always irritated beyond patience by the subject. I can remember her voice, a sort of faint minor chord, as she, lisping the "r" a little, uttered her remonstrating "Robert!" and his loud, dominant barytone sweeping away every possible plea she and my father could make; and then came my father's deliberate notes, which seemed to fall a little sadly—his voice always sounded a little sad—upon the rising waves of the discussion. I think this must have been just before we all went to Rome—it was in the morning, in some foreign city. I can see Mr. and Mrs. Browning, with their faces turned towards the window, and my father with his back to it, and all of us assembled in a little high-up room. Mr. Browning was dressed in a brown rough suit, and his hair was black hair then, and she, as far as I can remember, was, as usual, in soft-falling flounces of black silk, and with her heavy curls drooping, and a thin gold chain hanging round her neck.

In the winter of 1853–54 we lived in Rome, in the Via della Croce, and the Brownings lived in the Bocca di Leone, hard

---

* An ambiguous extract in Mrs. Orr's *Life of Browning* has only recalled my own most vivid impression of the happy relations between my father and Mrs. Browning.

by. The evenings our father dined away from home our old donna (so I think cooks used to be called) would conduct us to our tranquil dissipations, through the dark streets, past the swinging lamps, up and down the black stone staircases; and very frequently we spent an evening with Mrs. Browning in her quiet room, while Mr. Browning was out visiting some of the many friends who were assembled in Rome that year. At ten o'clock came our father's servant to fetch us back, with the huge key of our own somewhat imposing palazzo. It was a happy and an eventful time, all the more eventful and happy to us for the presence of the two kind ladies, Mrs. Browning and Mrs. Sartoris, who befriended us.

I can also remember one special evening at Mrs. Sartoris's, when a certain number of people were sitting just before dinner-time in one of those lofty Roman drawing-rooms, which become so delightful when they are inhabited by English people—which look so chill and formal in their natural condition. This saloon was on the first floor, with great windows at the farther end. It was all full of a certain mingled atmosphere, of flowers and light and comfort and color. It was in contrast but not out of harmony with Mrs. Browning's quiet room—in both places existed the individuality which real home-makers know how to give to their homes. Here swinging lamps were lighted up, beautiful things hung on the wall, the music came and went as it listed, a great piano was drawn out and open, the tables were piled with books and flowers. Mrs. Sartoris, the lady of the shrine, dressed in some flowing, pearly satin tea-gown, was sitting by a round-table reading to some other women who had come to see her. She was reading from a book of Mr. Browning's poems which had lately appeared; and as she read in her wonderful muse-like way she paused, she reread the words, and she emphasized the lines, then stopped short, the others exclaiming, half laughing, half protesting. . . . It was a lively, excitable party, outstaying the usual hour of a visit; questioning, puzzling, and discursive — a Browning society of the past—into the midst of which a door opens (and it is this fact which recalls it to my mind), and Mr. Browning himself walks in, and the burst of voices is suddenly reduced to one single voice, that of the hostess, calling him to her side, and asking him to define his meaning. But he evaded the question, began to talk of something else —he never much cared to talk of his own poetry—and the Browning society dispersed.

Mrs. Sartoris used to like to speak of a certain luncheon to which Mr. and Mrs. Browning once invited them when they were all staying in some country place in Italy, and which, so she always said, was one of the most delightful entertainments she could remember in all her life. One wonders whether the guests or the hosts contributed most. Each one has been happy and talked his or her best, and when the Sartorises got up reluctantly to go, saying, " How delightful it has been," Mr. Browning cried, " Come back to sup with us, do;" and Mrs. Browning exclaimed, "Oh, Robert, how can you ask them ! There is no supper, nothing but the remains of the pie." And then, cries Robert Browning, " Well, come back and finish the pie."

The *Pall Mall Gazette* of April 9, 1891, contains an amusing account of a journey from London to Paris taken forty years ago by Mr. and Mrs. Browning. The companion they carried with them writes of the expedition, dating from Chelsea, September 4, 1851 :

"The day before yesterday, near midnight, I returned from a very short and very insignificant excursion to Paris, which, after a month at Malvern water-cure and then a ten days at Scotsbrig, concludes my travels for this year. Miserable puddle and tumult all my travels are ; of no use to me except to bring agitation, sleeplessness, sorrow, and distress. Better not to travel at all unless when I am bound to do it. But this tour to Paris was a promised one. I had engaged to meet the Ashburtons (Lord and Lady) there, on their return from Switzerland and Hamburg, before either party left London. The time at last suited; all was ready except will on my part; so, after hesitation and painful indecision enough, I did resolve, packed my baggage again, and did the little tour I stood engaged for."

The chronicle begins on Monday, September 21st, when "Brother John" and Carlyle go to Chorley to consult about passports, routes, and conditions. . . .

"At Chapman's shop I learned that Robert Browning (poet) and his wife were just about setting out for Paris. I walked to their place; had, during that day and the following, consultations with these fellow-pilgrims, and decided to go with them *via* Dieppe on Thursday. . . .

"Up, accordingly, on Thursday morning, in unutterable flurry and tumult—phenomena on the Thames all dream-like, one spectralism chasing another—to the station in good time; found the Brownings just arriving, which seemed a good omen. Browning with wife and child and maid, then an empty seat for cloaks and baskets; lastly, at the opposite end from me, a hard-faced, honest Englishman or Scotchman all in gray with a gray cap, who looked rather ostrich-like, but proved very harmless and quiet—this was the loading of our carriage; and so away we went, Browning talking very loud and with vivacity, I silent rather, tending towards many thoughts. . . .

"Our friends, especially our French friends, were full of bustle, full of noise, at starting; but so soon as we had cleared the little channel of Newhaven, and got into the sea or British Channel, all this abated, sank into the general sordid torpor of sea-sickness, with its miserable noises—'houhah, hoh!'—and hardly any other, amid the rattling of the wind and sea. A sorry phasis of humanity! Browning was sick—lay in one of the bench tents horizontal, his wife below. I was not absolutely sick, but had to be quite quiet and without comfort, save in one cigar, for seven or eight hours of blustering, spraying, and occasional rain."

And so with mention of prostration into doleful silence, of evanition into utter darkness, of the poor Frenchman who was so lively at starting, the story continues:

"At Dieppe, while the others were in the hotel having some very bad cold tea and colder coffee, Browning was passing our luggage, brought it all in safe about half-past ten o'clock, and we could address ourselves to repose. So ' to bed in my upper room, bemoaned by the sea and small incidental noises of the harbor. . . . Next morning Browning, as before, did everything. I sat out-of-doors on some logs at my ease, and smoked, looking at the population and their ways. Browning fought for us, and we—that is, the woman, the child, and I—had only to wait and be silent.'. . . At Paris the travellers came into a ' crowding, jingling, vociferous tumult, in which the brave Browning fought for us, leaving me to sit beside the woman.'"

Mr. Browning once told us a little anecdote of the Carlyles at tea in Cheyne Row, and of Mrs. Carlyle pouring out the tea, while a brass kettle was boiling on the hob, and Mr. Browning, presently seeing that the kettle was needed and that Carlyle was not disposed to move, rose from his own chair, and filled the teapot for his hostess, and then stood by her tea-table still talking and absently holding the smoking kettle in his hand.

"Can't you put it down?" said Mrs. Carlyle, suddenly; and Mr. Browning, confused and somewhat absent, immediately popped the kettle down upon the carpet, which was a new one.

Mrs. Carlyle exclaimed in horror—I have no doubt she was half-laughing—"See how fine he has grown! He does not any longer know what to do with the kettle."

And, sure enough, when Mr. Browning penitently took it up again, a brown oval mark was to be seen clearly stamped and burned upon the new carpet. "You can imagine what I felt," said Mr. Browning. "Carlyle came to my rescue. 'Ye should have been more explicit,' said he to his wife."

VI

WHEN my father went for the second time to America, in 1856, my sister and I remained behind, and for a couple of days we stayed on in our home before going to Paris. Those days of parting are always sad ones, and we were dismally moping about the house and preparing for our own journey when we were immensely cheered by a visitor. It was Mr. Browning, who came in to see us, and who brought us an affectionate little note from his wife. We were to go and spend the evening with them, the kind people said. They had Mr. Kenyon's brougham at their disposal, and it would come and fetch us and take us back at night, and so that first sad evening passed far more happily than we could ever have imagined possible. I remember feeling, as young people do, utterly, hopelessly miserable, and then suddenly very cheerful every now and then. I believe my father had planned it all with them before he went away.

This was in the autumn of 1856, and *Aurora Leigh* was published in 1857. It was on the occasion of this journey home to England that the MS. of the poem was lost in a box at Marseilles.

In this same box were also carefully put away certain velvet suits and lace collars, in which the little son was to make his appearance among his English relatives. Who shall blame Mrs. Browning if her taste in boy's costume was somewhat too fanciful and poetic for the days in which she lived? At any rate, her chief concern was not for her

MR. MILSAND
From a copyrighted photograph by Julia Margaret Cameron

MSS., but for the loss of her little boy's wardrobe, which had been devised with so much motherly pride.

Happily for the world at large, one of Mrs. Browning's brothers chanced to pass through Marseilles, and the box was discovered by him stowed away in a cellar at the customs.

We must have met again in Paris later in this same year. The Brownings had an apartment near the Rond-Point, and we were living close by with our grandparents during my father's absence. We used frequently to go and see them, only to find again the same warm and tranquil atmosphere that we used to breathe at Rome—the sofa drawn out, the tiny lady in the corner, the sun dazzling in at the window. On one occasion Mr. Hamilton Aidé was paying a visit. He had been talking about books, and, half laughing, he turned to a young woman who had just come in, and asked her when *her* forthcoming work would be ready. Young persons are ashamed, and very properly so, of their early failures, of their *pattes de mouches* and wild attempts at authorship, and this one was no exception to the common law, and answered " Never," somewhat too emphatically. And then it was that Mr. Browning spoke one of those chance sayings which make headings to the chapters of one's life. " All in good time," he said, and he went on to ask us all if we remembered the epitaph on the Roman lady who sat at home, who spun wool. " You must spin your wool some day," he said, kindly, to the would-be authoress; " every woman has wool to spin of some sort or another; isn't it so?" he asked, and he turned to his wife.

I went home feeling quite impressed by the little speech, it had been so gravely and kindly made. My blurred pages looked altogether different somehow. It was spinning wool —it was not wasting one's time, one's temper—it was some-thing more than spoiling paper and pens. And this much I may perhaps add for the comfort of the future race of authoresses who are now twisting the cocoons from which the fluttering butterflies and Psyches yet to be will emerge some day upon their wings: never has anything given more trouble or seemed more painfully hopeless than those early incoherent pages, so full of meaning to one's self, so absolutely idiotic in expression. In later life the words come easily, only too readily; but then it is the meaning which lags behind.

It was in that same apartment that I remember hearing Mr. Browning say (across all these long years): "It may seem to you strange that such a thing as poetry should be written with regularity at the same hour in every day. But, nevertheless, I do assure you it is a fact that my wife and I sit down every morning after breakfast to our separate work; she writes in the drawing-room and I write in here," he said, opening a door into a little back empty room with a window over a court. And then he added, "I never read a word of hers until I see it all finished and ready for publication."

Among the people that belong to these old Paris days, there is one friend of very early date whom we used to meet from time to time with Mr. and Miss Browning at the house of Mrs. Corkran and elsewhere; this was Mr. Milsand, a man to whom every one turned with instinctive trust and sympathy, a slight body, a great and generous nature. Mr. Browning has described him in "Red Cotton Nightcap Country"—"a man of men" he calls him:

> "Talk to him for five minutes,
> Nonsense, sense, no matter what . . .
> There he stands, reads an English newspaper,
> Stock still, and now again upon the move
> Paces the beach, to taste the spring like you
> (Since both are human beings in God's eyes);
> That man will read you rightly head to foot."

A little further on follows a touching, outspoken expression of true feeling :

> " He knows more and loves better than the world
> That never heard his name and never may . . .
> What hinders that my heart relieve itself :
> ' O friend ! who makest warm my wintry world,
> And wise my heaven, if there we consort too.' "

To Mr. Milsand, Browning has dedicated one of the later editions of " Sordello " and others of his poems. By the kindness of Madame Milsand I am able to give some passages of Mr. Browning's correspondence with his friend. She has sent me the letters from her home at Dijon, and with the letters comes a little humorous sketch by the poet, of which a fac-simile is given here :

" FLORENCE, *February* 24, '58.

" It is far too many weeks now, my dear Milsand, since we got your letter—and certainly it has never been out of sight any more than out of mind, for I put it over the fireplace where we both sit these long winter evenings, and often, indeed, a glance at it has brought you beside us again, as on those pleasant Paris evenings. We English have a superstition that when people talk of us our *ears* burn — have yours caused you any serious inconvenience that way ? You know we three have long since passed the stage in friendship when assurances are necessary to any one of us. For us two here, we gained nothing by our sojourn in Paris like the knowledge and love of you, and yet Paris gave us many valuable things. One day, in all probability, we shall come together again, and meantime the news of you, though never so slight, will be a delight to us, yet your letter has been all this time unanswered ; but one reason was that only in the last day or two have I been able to get the review with your article in ; it is here on the table at last. In what is it obscure ? Strong, condensed, and direct it is, and no doubt the common readers of easy writing feel oppressed by twenty pages of such masculine stuff. . . . My wife will write a few lines about ourselves ; she is suffering a little from the cold which has come late, nor very severely either, but enough to influence her more than

I could wish. We live wholly alone here; I have not left the house one evening since our return. I am writing—a first step towards popularity for me—lyrics with more music and painting than before, so as to get people to hear and see . . . something to follow if I can compass it. . . .

"I have a new acquaintance here, much to my taste—Tennyson's eldest brother, who has long been settled here, with many of his brother's qualities: a very earnest, simple, and truthful man, with many admirable talents and acquirements, the whole sicklied o'er by an inordinate dose of our English disease, shyness; he sees next to no company, but comes here, and we walk together. . . . I knew too little of Mr. Darley.* Will he keep the slender memory of me he may have, and do you, dear Milsand, ever know me for yours affectionately,   R. B."

In this same letter there is a paragraph which runs as follows :

"Helen Faucit is going to produce an old play of mine, never acted, at the Haymarket, "Colombe's Birthday;" look out for it in April, keeping in mind the proverbial uncertainty of things theatrical. My main hope of its success lies in its being wholly an actor's and manager's speculation, not the writer's."

VII

It was in Florence Mrs. Browning wrote *Casa Guidi Windows*,† containing the wonderful description of the procession passing by, and that noble apostrophe to freedom beginning, "O! magi from East and from the West." *Aurora Leigh* was also written here, which the author herself calls "the most mature of her works," the one into which her

---

* The writer has left the little message to Mr. Darley, which commemorates another very early recollection: that of a gentle, handsome painter, whom she as a child remembers. His paintings made no particular impression upon us all, but his kind tranquillity of manner and courteous ways are not to be forgotten.

† See Biographical Dictionary.

highest convictions have entered. The poem is full of beauty from the first page to the last, and beats time to a noble human heart. The opening scenes in Italy; the impression of light, of silence; the beautiful Italian mother, the austere father, with his open books; the death of the mother, who lies laid out for burial in her red silk dress; the epitaph " weep for an infant too young to weep much, when Death removed this mother;" Aurora's journey to her father's old home; her lonely terror of England; her slow yielding to its silent beauty; her friendship with her cousin, Romney Leigh; their saddening, widening knowledge of the burden and sorrow of life, and the way this knowledge influences both their fates—all is described with that irresistible fervor which is the translation of the essence of things into words.

Mrs. Browning was a great writer; but I think she was even more a wife and a mother than a writer, and any account of her would be incomplete which did not put these facts first and foremost in her history.

The author of *Aurora Leigh* once added a characteristic page to one of her husband's letters to Leigh Hunt. She has been telling him of her little boy's illness. " You are aware that of that child I am more proud than twenty Auroras, even after Leigh Hunt has praised them. When he was ill he said to me, ' You pet, don't be unhappy about *me;* think it's only a boy in the street, and be a little sorry, but not unhappy.' Who could not be unhappy, I wonder? . . . I never saw your book called *The Religion of the Heart.* I receive more dogmas, perhaps (my ' perhaps ' being in the dark, rather), than you do."

She says in conclusion, " Churches do all of them, as at present constituted, seem too narrow and low to hold true Christianity in its proximate development—I, at least, cannot help believing them so."

She seemed, even in her life, something of a spirit, as her friend has said, and her view of life's sorrow and shame, of its beauty and eternal hope, is not unlike that which one might imagine a spirit's to be. She died at Florence in 1861. It is impossible to read without emotion the account of her last hours—given in *Robert Browning's Life*—of her tender, nay, playful courage and sweetness, of his passion of grief.

A tablet has been placed on Casa Guidi, voted by the municipality of Florence, and written by Tommaseo:

" Here wrote and died Elizabeth Barrett Browning, whose woman's heart combined the wisdom of a wise man with the genius of a poet, and whose poems form a golden ring which joins Italy to England. The town of Florence, ever grateful to her, has placed this epitaph to her memory."

There was a woman living in Florence, an old friend—clever, warm-hearted Miss Isa Blagden, herself a writer—who went to Mr. Browning and his little boy in their terrible desolation, and who did what little a friend could do to help them. Day after day, and for two or three nights, she watched by the stricken pair until she was relieved; then the father and the little son came back to England. They settled near Miss Barrett, Mrs. Browning's sister, who was living in Delamere Terrace, and upon her own father's death Miss Browning came to be friend, comforter, home-maker, for her brother.

I can remember walking with my father under the trees of Kensington Gardens, when we met Mr. Browning just after his return to England. He was coming towards us along the broad walk in his blackness through the sunshine. We were then living in Palace Green, close by, and he came to see us very soon after. But he was in a jarred and troubled state, and not himself as yet, although I remember his speaking of the house he had just taken for himself and his boy. This was only a short time before my father's death. In 1864 my sister and I left our home and went abroad, nor did we all meet again for a long time.

It was a mere chance, so Mr. Browning once said, whether he should live in this London house that he had taken, and join in social life, or go away to some quiet retreat, and be seen no more; but for great poets, as for small ones, events shape themselves by degrees, and after the first hard years of his return, a new and gentler day began to dawn for him. Miss Browning came to them, new interests arose, acquaintances ripened to friends (this blessed human fruit takes time to mature), his work and his influence spread.

He published some of his finest work about this time. *Dramatis Personæ*, a great part of which had been written before, came out in 1864; then followed the *Ring and the Book*, published by his good friend, and ours, Mr. George Murray Smith, and *Balaustion*, that exquisite poem, in 1871. Recognition, popularity, honorary degrees, all the tokens of appreciation, which should have come sooner, now began to crowd in upon "our great commoner," as some one called Mr. Browning when Lord Tennyson accepted his peerage—Lord Rectorships and Fellowships and dignities of every sort came in due course. He went his own way through it all, cordially accepted the recognition, but chiefly avoided the dignities, and kept his two lives distinct. He had his public life and his own private life, with its natural interests and outcoming friendships, and constant alternate pulse of work and play.

Browning has been described as looking something like a hale naval officer; but in later life, when his hair turned snowy white, he seemed to me more like some sage of bygone ages. There was a statue in the Capitol of Rome to which Mrs. Sartoris always likened him. I cannot imagine that any draped and filleted sage could ever have been so delightful a companion, so racy, so unselfishly interested in the events of the hour as he. "He was not only ready for talk, but fond of it," said the writer of an admirable article in the *Standard*.* "He was absolutely unaffected in his choice of topics: anything but the cant of literary circles pleased him. If only we knew a tithe of what he knew, and of what, unluckily, he gives us credit for knowing, many a hint that serves only to obscure the sense would be clear enough."

Among Browning's many gifts, that of delightful story-telling is certainly one which should not be passed over. His memory was very remarkable for certain things; general facts, odds and ends of rhyme and doggerel, bits of recondite knowledge came back to him spontaneously and with vivacity. This is all to be noticed in his books, which treat of so many quaint facts and theories. His stories were specially delightful, because they were told so appo-

* To quote the many voices as they speak of him is to quote the voices of a whole host of friends and followers in the spirit or the letter. Guided by Mr Furnival I have read a cycle of commentaries, among which I should like to mention two articles in the *Jewish Quarterly Review*, which seem to me specially interesting. "Browning is a poet for the old as well as for the young. Some poets write of summer, others of spring. Browning belongs even more to wintry times, or to the early silent months which precede the spring. The branches of the trees may be dry and frozen, but in them lies the sap of hope and life, the frost-bound earth contains the harvests of the year, its joys and fragrance and sweetness to be. Who more than Browning has ever made us realize that life which exists alongside with death, that truth and law which underlies confusion. 'I press God's lamp close to my breast, its splendor soon or late will pierce the gloom.'" Sir James Fitz James Stephen, in his "Essay on Hooker," quotes a passage which might almost serve for a motto to some of Browning's finest work. "In all created and imperfect beings there is an appetite and desire whereby they incline to something which they may be, which as yet they are not in act.

" 'So in man's life arise
August anticipations, symbols, types
Of a dim splendor ever on before,
In that eternal circle life pursues.' "—PARACELSUS.

And again, "That which doth assign to each thing the kind, that which doth moderate the force and power, that which doth appoint the form and measure of working, the same we term a law." Again hear Paracelsus:

" But thou shalt painfully attain to joy
While hope and fear and love shall keep thee man."

sitely, and were so simple and complete in themselves. A doggerel always had a curious fascination for him, and he preferred to quote the very worst poetry in his talks. On one occasion we were dining at Mr. and Mrs. Lehmann's house in Half-moon Street: it was a cottage of delight rather than a palace, and the guests were somewhat crowded. Millais, turning round, happened to brush off the head of a flower that Browning wore in his button-hole. Concerning the said flower, the poet immediately remembered a story of a city clerk who had considered himself inspired, and had some of his verses printed. One poem began something like this :

> " I love the gentle primrose
>   That grows beside the rill ;
> I love the water-lily,
>   Narcissus, and jonquil."

This last word was by mistake printed " John Quill," which seemed so appropriate a name, and the clerk got so much chaffed about it, that his poetical inspirations were nipped in the bud, and he printed no more poems.

Another reminiscence which my friend Mrs. C—— also recalls is in a sadder strain. It was a description of something Mr. Browning once saw in Italy. It happened at Arezzo, where he had turned by chance into an old church among the many old churches there, that he saw a crowd of people at the end of an aisle, and found they were looking at the skeleton of a man just discovered by some workmen who were breaking away a portion of the wall opposite the high altar. The flesh was like brown leather, but the features were distinguishable. Mr. Browning made inquiries as to who it was. He could hear of no tradition even of a man being walled up. The priests thought it must have been done three or four hundred years ago. A hole had been left above his head to enable him to breathe. Mr. Browning said the dead man was standing with his hands crossed upon his breast; on the face was a look of expectation, an expression of hoping against hope. The man looked up, knowing help could only come from above, and must have died still hoping. Mrs. C—— said to Mr. Browning she wondered he had not written a poem about it. He replied he *had* done so, and had given it away.

I often find myself going back to Darwin's saying about the duration of a man's friendships being one of the best measures of his worth, and Browning's friendships are very characteristic and convincing. He specially loved Landor, to whom he and his wife were Good Samaritans indeed. For the Tennysons his was also a real and warm affection. Was there ever a happier, truer dedication than that of his collected selections?—

"TO ALFRED TENNYSON:

"In poetry illustrious and consummate. In friendship noble and sincere!"

How enduring was his friendship for Mr. Procter, and how often has his faithful coming cheered the dear and kind old man! Of his feeling for Mr. Milsand I have already spoken. Among the women who were Mr. Browning's real and confidential friends there is the same feeling of trust and dependence.   170

VIII

BESIDES actual personal feelings, there are also the Affinities of a life to be taken into account. The following passages, which I owe to Professor Knight's kindness, are very remarkable, for they show what Browning's estimation was of Wordsworth, and although they were not written till much later, I give them here. Indeed, the point of meeting of these two beneficent poet streams is one full of interest to those upon the shore. The first paragraph of the first letter relates to some new honors and dignities gratefully and firmly declined :

"March 21st, '83.

"I *do* feel increasingly (cowardly as seems the avowal) the need of keeping the quiet corner in the world's van which I have got used to for so many years.

"I will, as you desire, attempt to pick out the twenty poems which strike me (and so as to take away my breath) as those worthiest of the master Wordsworth.

"Speaking of a classification of Wordsworth's poems, in my heart I fear I should do it almost chronologically, so immeasurably superior seem to me the first sprightly runnings ; your selection would appear to be excellent, and the partial admittance of the latter work prevents one from observing the too definitely distinguishing black line between supremely good and—well ! what is fairly tolerable from Wordsworth always understand."

At the end of the letters addressed to Professor Knight there is this touching postscript :

"I open the envelope to say—what I had nearly omitted—that Ld. Coleridge proposed, and my humble self—at his desire—seconded you, last evening, for admission to the Athenæum. I had the less scruple in offering my services that you will most likely never see in the offer anything but a record of my respect and regard, since your election will come on when I shall be—dare I hope?—'elect' in even a higher society!"

Here is another letter also relating to Wordsworth:

"19 WARWICK CRESCENT, W.,
February 24, '86.

"MY DEAR PROFESSOR,—I have kept you waiting this long while—and for how shabby a result! You must listen indulgently while I attempt to explain why I am forced to disappoint you. One remembers few more commonplace admonitions to a poet than that 'he would wiselier have written but a quarter of the works which he has labored at for a lifetime,' unless it be this other, often coupled with it, 'that such works ought to be addressed to the general apprehension, not exclusively suited to the requirements of a (probably quite imaginary) few.' Each precept contradicts the other. Write, on set purpose, for the many, and you will soon enough be reminded of the old 'Tot homines;' and write as conscientiously for the few—your idealized 'Double' (it comes to that)—and you may soon suit him with the extremely little that suits yourself. Now in view of which of these objects should the maker of a selection of the works of any poet worth the pains begin his employment?

"I have myself attempted the business, and know something of the achievements in this kind of my betters. They furnish a list of the pieces which the selector has found most delight in. And I have found also, that others, playing the selector with apparently as good a right and reason, were dissatisfied with this unaccountable addition, and that as inexplicable omission; in short, that the sole selector was not himself. The only case in which no such stumbling-block occurs being that obvious one—if it has ever occurred—when a public, wholly unacquainted with an author, is presumed to be accessible to a specimen of his altogether untried productions—for, by chance, the sample of the poetry of Brown and Jones may pierce the ignorance of somebody—say of Robinson. It is quite another matter of interest to know what Matthew Arnold thinks most worthy in Wordsworth. But should anybody have curiosity to inquire which 'fifteen or twenty' of his poems have most thoroughly impressed such a one as myself, all I can affirm is that I treasure as precious every poem written during about the first twenty years of the poet's life; after these, the solution grows weaker, the crystals gleam more rarely, and the assiduous stirring up of the mixture is too apparent and obtrusive. To the end crystals are to be come at; but my own experience resembles that of the old man in the admirable 'Resolution and Independence:'

> "'Once I could meet with them on every side,
>   But they have dwindled long by slow decay,
>   Yet still I persevere, and find them where I may'

—that is, in the poet's whole work, which I should leave to operate in the world as it may, each recipient his own selector.

"I only find room to say that I was delighted to make acquaintance with your daughter, and that should she feel any desire to make that of my sister, we shall welcome her gladly.

"Believe me, my dear Professor,

"Yours most truly,

"ROBERT BROWNING."

IX

WE were all living in "sea-coast-nook-full" Normandy one year, scattered into various châteaus and shops and tenements. Some of our party were installed in a clematis-wreathed mansion near the church-tower; others were at the milk-woman's on the road to the sea. Most of the lively population of the little watering-place was stowed away in châlets of which the fronts seemed wide open to the road from morning to night; numbers of people contentedly spent whole days in tents on the sea-shore. It was a fine hot summer, with sweetness and completeness everywhere; the cornfields gilt and far-stretching, the waters blue, the skies arching high and clear, and the sunsets suc ceeding each other, in most glorious light and beauty. Mr. Milsand had a little country lodge at St. Aubin, near Luc-sur-Mer, and I wrote to him from the shady court-yard of our château, and begged him to come over and see us; and when he came he told us Mr. and Miss Browning were also living close by. We were walking along the dusty road and passing the old square tower when he suddenly stood still, and, fixing his earnest look upon me, said:

"Tell me, why is there some reserve; is anything wrong between you and Robert Browning? I see you are re-served; I see he is also constrained; what is it?"

To which I replied, honestly enough, that I did not know what it was; there *was* some constraint between me and my old friend. I imagined that some one had made mis-chief; I could see plainly enough when we met that he was changed and vexed and hurt, but I could not tell why, and it certainly made me very unhappy. "But this must not be," said Milsand; "this must be cleared." I said it was hope-less; it had lasted for months, and in those days I was still young enough to imagine that a mood was eternal; that coldness could never change. Now I find it almost impos-sible to give that consideration to a quarrel which is inva-riably claimed under such circumstances.

I happened to be alone next day; the cousins and the children who were with me had gone down to the sea. I was keeping house in the blazing heat with F—— (the family despot, the late nurse and present house-keeper of the party). The shutters were closed against the blinding light; I was writing in my bedroom, with a pleasant sense of temporary solitude and silence, when I chanced to go to the window, and looked into the old walled court. I saw the great gates open a little way, and a man's broad-shoul-dered figure coming through them, and then advance, strid-ing across the stones, towards the house. It was Mr.

Browning, dressed all in white, with a big white umbrella under his arm. It was the poet himself, and over and beyond this, it was my kind, *old* friend returned, all reserve and coldness gone, never to trouble or perplex again. We had no explanations.

"Don't ask," he said; "the facts are not worth remembering or inquiring into; people make mischief without even meaning it. It is all over now. I have come to ask when you will come to St. Aubin; my sister is away for a few days, but the Milsands are counting on you."

We started almost the next day in a rattle-trap chaise, with an escort of donkeys ridden by nephews and nieces, along the glaring sandy road to Luc. The plains were burning hot and the sea seemed on fire, but the children and donkeys kept up valiantly. At last we reached a little village on the outer edges of Luc-sur-Mer, and in the street stood Monsieur Milsand, in front of a tiny house. How kind was his greeting! How cordial was that of his wife and daughter, coming to the door to make us welcome! Mr. Browning was also waiting in the diminutive sitting-room, where I remember a glimpse of big books and comfortable seats and tables. The feast itself was spread out-of-doors on the terrace at the back, with a shady view of the sea between lilac-bushes: the low table was laid with dainties, glasses, and quaint decanters. Mr. Milsand was the owner of vineyards in the South, and abstemious though he was himself, he gave his friends the best of good wine, as well as of words and welcome. From this by-gone and happy feast two dishes are still present to my mind: a certain capon and a huge fish, lying in a country platter, curled on a bed of fennel, surrounded by a wreath of marigolds, and in its mouth a bunch of flowers. The host helped us each in turn; the Normandy maid appeared and disappeared with her gleaming gold ear-rings; then came a pause, during which Madame Milsand rose quietly, and went into the house. The gentlemen were talking pleasantly, and the ladies listening agreeably (there are many local politics to be discussed on the Normandy coast). But somehow, after a time, the voices ceased, and in the silence we heard the strains of distant martial music. Mr. Milsand looked inquiringly at his daughter.

"It is the regiment marching by," said Mlle. Milsand.

"But where is my wife?" said Monsieur Milsand. "*She* cannot have gone to the review."

Still the music sounded; still we waited. Then to us returned our handsome, dignified hostess. "She had not been to the review," she said, laughing and apologizing; "but, ladies and gentlemen," she added, "you must please content yourselves with your fricandeau, for, alas! there is no news of my larded capon. It went to the pastry-cook's to be roasted; I have just sent the maid to inquire; it was despatched, ready for the table, half an hour ago, on a tray carried by the pastry-cook's boy. It is feared that it is running after the soldiers. I am in despair at your meagre luncheon."

But I need not say we were in a land flowing with milk and honey. As we feasted on, as the last biscuit was crumbled, the last fragrant cup of coffee handed round, once more came the Normandy ear-rings.

"Shall I serve the capon, madame? Pierre has just returned from the review."

But we all cried out that we must come back another day to eat the capon. The sun was getting low. If we carried out our intention of walking to St. Aubin and seeing Mr. Browning's cottage, we must start forthwith.

The path ran along the high cliff. Mr. Browning went before us, leading the way to "mine own hired house." Once more the whole scene comes before me: the sea-coast far below our feet, the arid vegetation of the sandy way, the rank, yellow snap-dragons lining the paths. There was not much other color: the tones were delicate, half airy, half solid; the sea was in a vast circle around us; the waves were flowing into the scooped sandy bay of Luc-sur-Mer; the rocks of the Calvados were hidden behind the jutting promontories; here and there a rare poppy, like a godsend, shone up by chance. It took us half an hour's quick walk to reach the two little straight sentry-boxes standing on the cliffs against the sky, to which Mr. Browning pointed. He himself has described this habitation in "Red Cotton Nightcap Country:"

> "That just behind you is mine own hired house,
>   With right of pathway through the field in front.
>   No prejudice to all its growth unsheath'd
>   Of emerald Luzern bursting into blue. . . .
>   Be sure I keep the path that hugs the wall
>   Of mornings, as I pad from door to gate!
>   Yon yellow—what if not wild-mustard flower?
>   Of that my naked sole makes lawful prize,
>   Bruising the acrid aromatics out . . .
>   And lo, the wave protrudes a lip at last,
>   And flecks my foot with froth, nor tempts in vain."

We entered the Brownings' house. The sitting-room door opened to the garden and the sea beyond—a fresh-swept bare floor, a table, three straw chairs, one book upon the table. Mr. Browning told us it was the only book he had with him. The bedrooms were as bare as the sitting-room, but I remember a little dumb piano standing in a corner, on which he used to practise in the early morning. I heard Mr. Browning declaring they were perfectly satisfied with their little house. That his brains, squeezed as dry as a sponge, were only ready for fresh air.

But has not Browning himself best summed up the contrast between the meek, hitherto un-Murrayed bathing-place and London, where

"My toe trespassed upon your flounce,
  Small blame unto you, seeing the staircase party in the square
  Was small and early, and you broke no rib."

X

THIS visit to St. Aubin was followed by the publication of " Red Cotton Nightcap Country," from which I have been quoting, and on this occasion I must break my rule, and trench upon the ground traversed by Mrs. Orr. I cannot give myself greater pleasure than by inserting the following passage from the *Life:*

"The August of 1872 and of 1873 again found him and his sister at St. Aubin, and the earlier visit was an important one, since it supplied him with the materials of his next work, of which Miss Annie Thackeray, there also for a few days, suggested the title. The tragic drama which forms the subject of Mr. Browning's poem had been in great part nacted in the vicinity of St. Aubin, and the case of disputed inheritance to which it had given rise was pending at that moment in the tribunals of Caen. The prevailing impression left on Miss Thackeray's mind by this primitive district was, she declared, that of white cotton nightcaps (the habitual head-gear of the Normandy peasants). She engaged to write a story called 'White Cotton Nightcap Country,' and Mr. Browning's quick sense of both contrast and analogy inspired the introduction of this element of repose into his own picture of that peaceful, prosaic existence, and of the ghostly, spiritual conflict to which it had served as background."

And perhaps the writer may be excused for adding a letter which concerns the dedication of " Red Cotton Night-

" Some have been ticketed like this knowingly
The shore he Spanish or native's laughter " —
— You're; the little patch I wished to
the toe-piece of this slipper seemed to
tickle by comparison.

Ever yours affectionately
Robert Browning,

cap Country"—a very unexpected and delightful consequence of our friendly meeting:

"*May* 9, 1873

"DEAR MISS THACKERAY,—Indeed the only sort of pain that any
sort of criticism could give me would be by the reflection of any particle
of pain it managed to give *you*. I dare say that, by long use, I don't
feel or attempt to feel criticisms of this kind, as most people might.
Remember that everybody this thirty years has given me his kick and
gone his way, just as I am told the understood duty of all highway travellers in Spain is to bestow at least one friendly thump for the Mayoral's
sake on his horses as they toil along up-hill, 'so utterly a puzzle,' 'or-
gan-grinding,' and so forth, come and go again without much notice ; but
any poke at me which would touch *you*, would vex me indeed ; therefore pray don't let my critics into *that* secret ! Indeed, *I* thought the
article highly complimentary, which comes of being in the category celebrated by Butler :

"'Some have been kicked till they know [not] whether
    The shoe be Spanish or neat's leather.'

"You see the little patch of velvet in the toe-piece of this slipper
seemed to tickle by comparison. Ever yours affectionately,
"ROBERT BROWNING."

But, whatever the past may have contained, Mr. Browning
had little to complain of in his future critics. This is not
an unappreciative age ; the only fault to be found with it is
that there are too many mouths using the same words over
and over again, until the expressions seem to lose their
senses and fly about almost giddily and at hap-hazard. The
extraordinary publicity in which our bodies live seems to
frighten away our souls at times ; we are apt to stick to
generalities, or to well-hackneyed adjectives which have
ceased to have much meaning or responsibility ; or if we
try to describe our own feelings, it is in terms which sometimes grow more and more emphatic as they are less and
less to the point. When we come to say what is our simple

and genuine conviction, the effort is almost beyond us. We remember so many clever confusing things that other people have said. The truth is too like Cordelia's. To say that you have loved a man or a woman, that you admire them and delight in their work, does not any longer mean to you or to others what it means in fact. It seems almost a test of Mr. Browning's true greatness that the love and the trust in his genius have survived the things which have been said about it.

XI

NOT the least interesting part of the Milsand correspondence relates to the MSS. which the cultivated Frenchman now regularly revised for his English friend before they were sent to the printer. Here is a letter to Mr. Milsand, dated May, 1872: "Whenever you get the whole series," Browning says, "you will see what I fail to make you understand, how *inestimable* your assistance has been; there is not one point to which you called attention which I was not thereby enabled to improve, in some cases essentially benefit; the punctuation was nearly as useful as the other apparently more important assistance. The fact is that in the case of a writer with my peculiarities and habits, somebody quite ignorant of what I may have meant to write, and only occupied with what is really written, is needed to supervise the thing produced, and I never hoped or dreamed that I should find such intelligence as yours at my service. I won't attempt to thank you, dearest friend, but simply in my own interest do not you undervalue your service to me, because in logical consequence the next step ought to be that you abate it or withdraw it." In another letter, dated

Dear Mr. Thackeray, you asked me too
long ago for a 'contribution' to your
magazine — too long ago in every
sense perhaps — for here is my
husband who suggests that, being in
very ill odour with you all in
England just now, (scarcely bettered
by a misstatement in the Athenaeum)
I may not be welcome between
the wind & your nobility at
Cornhill —

But in that case you will
return my verses enclosed, &
no harm will be done — if
indeed it is no harm to send

love to dear Annie & Minnie ..
whom I never forget.

Yes, — and don't I remember
Mr. Thackeray's kindness to
little Penini — who grows
big, & is learning Latin, &
riding a poney, & is not much
changed otherwise —

With my husband's regards,
I remain ..
most sincerely yours
Elizabeth Barrett Browning

28. Via del Tritone —
Rome — April 13 —
Where we shall be till the
end of May — Then we return
to Florence —

1875, Mr. Browning writes again about punctuation. " Your way of punctuation (French way) is different from ours—I don't know why; we use -:-where you prefer -;- but I have Frenchified myself in this respect for your sake." " I know how I trouble all but your goodness," he repeats to his friend. Is it not a pleasure to think of the records in the old carved house at Dijon; of the good service rendered, and so generously acknowledged?

Here is one more extract from the Dijon correspondence, dated April 7, 1878: " I am glad you like the poems. The measures were hitherto unused by me. That of the first poems is

and the cæsura falls just as you say, and should, as a rule, be strictly observed, but to prevent monotony, I occasionally break it." This letter concludes by an allusion to a French friend who is learning English, and speaking of the difficulties of a foreign tongue, Mr. Browning says: " The thoughts outstrip and leave behind the words; in the slower process of writing, the thought is compelled to wait, and get itself suited in a phrase." " Now for yourself," he concludes, " I enjoy altogether your enjoyment of Bébé, and wish that grand'mère may be tyrannized over more and more Turkishly. It is the good time. Give my true love to whoever will take it of your joyous party. Sarianna writes often, I know. We hail the announcement of your speedy arrival as ever."

The house by the water-side, in Warwick Crescent, which Browning hastily took, and in which he lived for so many years after his return to England, was a very charming corner, I used to think. It was London, but London touched by some indefinite romance: the canal used to look cool and deep, the green trees used to shade the crescent; it seemed a peaceful oasis after crossing that dreary Æolia of Paddington, with its many despairing shrieks and whirling eddies. The house was an ordinary London house, but the carved oak furniture and tapestries gave dignity to the long drawing-rooms, and pictures and books lined the stairs. In the garden at the back dwelt, at the time of which I am writing, two weird gray geese, with quivering silver wings and long throats, who used to come to meet their master hissing and fluttering. When I said I liked the place, he told us of some visitor from abroad, who had lately come to see him, who also liked Warwick Crescent, and who, looking up and down the long row of houses and porticos in front of the canal, said, "Why, this is a mansion, sir; do you inhabit the whole of this great building, and do you allow the public to sail upon the water?"

As we sat at luncheon I looked up and down the room, with its comfortable lining of books, and also I could not help noticing the chimney-board heaped with invitations. I never saw so many cards in my life before. Lothair himself might have wondered at them.

Mr. Browning talked on, not of the present London, but of Italy and *villeggiatura*, with his friends, the Storys; of Siena days and of Walter Savage Landor. He told us the piteous story of the old man wandering forlorn down the street in the sunshine without a hole to hide his head. He kindled at the remembrance of the old poet, of whom he said his was the most remarkable personality he had ever known; and then, getting up abruptly from the table, he reached down some of Landor's many books from the shelves near the fireplace, declaring he knew no finer reading.

He read us some extracts from the "Conversations with the Dead," quickly turning over the leaves, seeking for his favorite passages.

There is a little anecdote which I think he also told us on this occasion. It concerned a ring which he used to wear, and which had belonged to his wife. One day in the Strand he discovered that the intaglio from the setting was missing. People were crowding in and out, there seemed no chance of recovering; but all the same he retraced his steps, and lo! in the centre of the crossing, there lay the jewel on a stone, shining in the sun. He had lost the ring on a previous occasion in Florence and found it there by another happy chance.

XII

It was not until 1887 that Mr. Browning moved to De Vere Gardens, where I saw him almost for the last time. I remember calling there at an early hour with my children. The servant hesitated about letting us in. Kind Miss Browning came out to speak to us, and would not hear of us going away.

"Wait a few minutes. I know he will see you," she said. "Come in. Not into the dining-room; there are some ladies waiting there; and there are some members of the Browning Society in the drawing-room. Robert is in the study, with some Americans who have come by appointment. Here is my sitting-room," she said; "he will come to you directly."

We had not waited five minutes, when the door opened wide, and Mr. Browning came in. Alas! it was no longer the stalwart visitor from St. Aubin. He seemed tired, hurried, though not less outcoming and cordial, in his silver age.

"Well, what can I do for you?" he said, dropping into a chair, and holding out both his hands.

I told him it was a family festival, and that I had "brought the children to ask for his blessing."

"Is that all?" he said, laughing, with a kind look, not without some relief. He also hospitably detained us, and when his American visitors were gone, took us in turn up into his study, where the carved writing-tables were covered with letters—a milky way of letters, it seemed to me, flowing in from every direction.

"What! all this to answer?" I exclaimed.

"You can have no conception what it is," he replied. "I am quite worn out with writing letters by the time I begin my day's work."

But his day's work was ending here. In the autumn of the year 1889 he went to Italy, and from Asolo wrote a happy and delightful letter to his brother-in-law, Mr. George Barrett, describing the "ancient city older than Rome," the immense indescribable charm of the surrounding country—the Alps on one side, the Asolan Mountains all round, and opposite the vast Lombard Plains. . . . "We think of leaving in a week or two," so he says, for Venice—guests of Pen and his wife. He writes of his children, and of his and his sister's happiness in their beautiful home, and also of the new edition of the works of "E. B. B." He seemed well when he first reached Venice, but it was winter even in Venice, Mrs. Orr says, and taking his usual walk on the Lido he caught cold. Attacks of faintness set in, and two hours before midnight on Thursday, December 12th, he breathed his last, closing his eyes in his son's beautiful home at Venice among those he loved best. His son, his sister, his daughter-in-law, were round about his bed tending and watching to the last. When all was over, they brought him home to England to rest.

When Spenser died in the street in Westminster, in which

he dwelt after his home in Ireland was burned and his child was killed by the rebels, it is said, that after lingering in this world in poverty and neglect, he was carried to the grave in state, and that his sorrowing brother-poets came and stood round about his grave, and each in turn flung in an ode to his memory, together with the pen with which it had been written. The present Dean of Westminster, quoting this story, added that probably Shakespeare had stood by the grave with the rest of them, and that Shakespeare's own pen might still be lying in dust in the vaults of the old abbey. There is something in the story very striking to the imagination. One pictures to one's self the gathering of those noble dignified men of the Elizabethan age, whose thoughts were at once so strong and so gentle, so fierce and so tender, whose dress was so elaborate and stately. Perhaps in years to come people may imagine to themselves the men who stood only the other day round Robert Browning's grave, the friends who loved him, the writers who have written their last tribute to this great and generous poet. There are still some eagles' quills among us; there are others of us who have not eagles' quills to dedicate to his memory, only nibs with which to pen a feeling, happily stronger and more various than the words and scratches which try to speak of it: a feeling common to all who knew him, and who loved the man of rock and sunshine, and who were proud of his great gift of spirit and of his noble human nature.

It often happens when a man dies in the fulness of years, that as you look across his grave, you can almost see his lifetime written in the faces gathered round about it. There stands his history. There are his companions and his early associates and those who loved him, and those with whom his later life was passed. You may hear the voices that have greeted him, see the faces he last looked upon; you may even go back and find some impression of early youth in the young folks who recall a past generation to those who remember the past. And how many phases of a long and varied life must have been represented in the great procession which followed Robert Browning to his honored grave! passing along the London streets and moving on through the gloomy fog, assembling from many a distant place to show respect to one

> "Who never turned his back, but marched breast forward,
> Never doubted clouds would break;
> Never dreamed, tho' right were worsted,
> Wrong would triumph.
> Held—we fall to rise, are baffled to fight better,
> Sleep to wake."

THE END

SOME LITERARY BIOGRAPHIES.

Boswell's Life of Johnson, including Boswell's Journal of a Tour to the Hebrides, and Johnson's Diary of a Journey into North Wales. Edited by GEORGE BIRKBECK HILL, D.C.L., Pembroke College, Oxford. *Popular Edition.* 6 volumes. Cloth, Uncut Edges and Gilt Tops, $10 00.

Letters of Samuel Johnson, LL.D. Collected and Edited by GEORGE BIRKBECK HILL, D.C.L., Pembroke College, Oxford; Editor of Boswell's "Life of Johnson." 2 volumes. With a fac-simile letter. 8vo, Cloth, Uncut Edges and Gilt Tops, $7 50.

The Correspondence of John Lothrop Motley, D.C.L. Edited by GEORGE WILLIAM CURTIS. With Portrait. 2 volumes. Royal 8vo, Cloth, Uncut Edges, Gilt Tops, $7 00; Sheep, $8 00; Half Calf, $11 50.

The Journal of Sir Walter Scott, 1825–1832. From the Original Manuscript at Abbotsford. With Two Portraits and Engraved Title-pages. 2 volumes. 8vo, Cloth, Uncut Edges and Gilt Tops, $7 50; Half Calf, $12 00. *Popular Edition.* 2 vols. in 1. Crown 8vo, Cloth, $2 50.

Memoir of the Life of Laurence Oliphant and of Alice Oliphant, his wife. By MARGARET OLIPHANT W. OLIPHANT. With Two Photogravure Portraits. 2 volumes. Crown 8vo, Cloth, Uncut Edges and Gilt Tops, $7 00.

A Sketch of the Life and Times of the Rev. Sydney Smith, M.A. (Rector of Combe-Florey, and Canon Residentiary of St. Paul's). Based on Family Documents and the Recollections of Personal Friends. By STUART J. REID. With Steel-plate Portraits, Numerous Illustrations, and Autograph Letter. 8vo, Cloth, $3 00.

The Life, Letters, and Literary Remains of Edward Bulwer, Lord Lytton. By his Son, the EARL OF LYTTON ("Owen Meredith"). Volume I. (containing Vols. I. and II. of the English Edition). Illustrated. 12mo, Cloth, $2 75.

The Life and Letters of Lord Macaulay. By his Nephew, GEORGE OTTO TREVELYAN, M.P. With Portrait on Steel. *Library Edition.* 2 volumes. 8vo, Cloth, Uncut Edges and Gilt Tops, $5 00; Half Calf, $9 50. *Popular Edition.* Complete in one volume, 12mo, Cloth, $1 75.

Letters and Memorials of Jane Welsh Carlyle. Prepared for Publication by THOMAS CARLYLE. Edited by JAMES ANTHONY FROUDE. 12mo, Cloth, $1 00.

Life of Thomas Carlyle. By JAMES ANTHONY FROUDE, M.A. Part I. A History of the First Forty Years of Carlyle's Life (1795-1835). With Illustrations. 12mo, Cloth, $1 00.—Part II. A History of Carlyle's Life in London (1834-1881). Illustrated. 12mo, Cloth, $1 00.

Thomas Carlyle. By M. D. CONWAY. Illustrated. 12mo, Cloth, $1 00.

What I Remember. By THOMAS ADOLPHUS TROLLOPE. 2 volumes. 12mo, Cloth, $1 75 each.

Memoirs of a Man of the World. Fifty Years of London Life. By EDMUND YATES. Portrait. 12mo, Cloth, $1 75.

An Autobiography. By ANTHONY TROLLOPE. With Portrait. 12mo, Cloth, $1 25.

Some Literary Recollections. By JAMES PAYN. With a Portrait. 12mo, Cloth, $1 00.

My Autobiography and Reminiscences. By W. P. FRITH, R.A. Portraits. 2 vols., 12mo, Cloth, $1 50 each.

Charles Reade, D.C.L., Dramatist, Novelist, Journalist. A Memoir compiled chiefly from his Literary Remains. By CHARLES L. READE, and the Rev. COMPTON READE. With Portrait. 12mo, Cloth, $1 25.

George Eliot's Life, as Related in her Letters and Journals. Arranged and Edited by her Husband, J. W. CROSS. Portraits and Illustrations. In Three Volumes. Library Edition, 12mo, Cloth, $3 75; Half Calf, $9 00. *Popular Edition,* 12mo, Cloth, $2 25. Special Edition in 3 vols., Half Cloth Binding, $2 00.

Autobiography of Henry Taylor. 1800-1875. In Two Volumes. With Portrait. 8vo, Cloth, $3 00.

English Men of Letters. Edited by JOHN MORLEY. 12mo, Cloth, 75 cents per volume. Thirty-eight volumes now ready. *Popular Edition.* 36 volumes in 12, Cloth, $12 00; Half Leather, $21 00.

PUBLISHED BY HARPER & BROTHERS, NEW YORK.

☞ *The above works are for sale by all booksellers, or will be sent by* HARPER & BROTHERS, *postage prepaid, to any part of the United States, Canada, or Mexico, on receipt of the price.*

www.ingramcontent.com/pod-product-compliance
Lightning Source LLC
Chambersburg PA
CBHW030537040726
47497CB00008B/2494